Contents

1

Creating Simple Database Tables

*Display field names
or more readable
captions*

*Specify what data
must be entered and
how it should look*

				Employees			4/18/94	

Emp#	SS#	First Name	Last Name	Address	City	Zip	Phone#	First Day
002	796-29-4473	Carol	Talbot	1109 Emerson Way	Lakewood	11403	334-7625	27-Aug-79
019	228-12-9111	Ron	Westerman	1419 Ivy Drive	Pinedale	11415	335-1326	08-Sep-85
027	854-72-2249	Fred	Anderson	943 Spruce Circle	Lakewood	11403	832-8779	14-Feb-89
029	934-21-8635	James	Murray	7921 Port Avenue	Lakewood	11403	834-5934	22-Mar-91
033	583-02-1253	Lance	Bright	148 Center St., #B211	Pinedale	11415	334-6683	23-Jun-91
034	477-11-6309	Richard	Talbot	1109 Emerson Way	Lakewood	11403	334-7625	23-Jun-91
035	722-52-2624	Linda	Gardner	8841 Market Street	Lakewood	11403	334-6754	02-May-92
038	241-21-4972	Jonathan	Bray	5941 Hilltop Road	Lakewood	11403	334-0180	17-Jun-92

*Use field proper-
ties to determine
a field's format*

Page 1

*Change how
information looks
onscreen, but not
the underlying data*

*Specify default
entries to speed up
data input*

You have probably just installed Microsoft Access for Windows and are excited but nervous about learning to use this powerful database tool. You are hoping that, like other Windows applications, Access will be simple to use and yet offer you the power you need to handle complex data. Well, relax. By the end of this chapter, you will know how to create database tables, enter data, and move around. If you have used other database applications, a quick review of this chapter will get you moving.

Throughout this book, we focus on how to use Access to carry out common database tasks, and for our examples, we show you how to create a database for a small roofing contractor. You will easily be able to adapt these examples to your particular needs. Because good database design is essential if you want to take maximum advantage of Access, from time to time we'll discuss design philosophy. We won't be able to cover this topic in detail, but a few pointers along the way will help you design your databases more efficiently.

Database design →

We assume that you have already installed both Windows 3.1 and Access 2 for Windows on your computer. We also assume that you've worked with Windows before and that you know how to start programs, move windows, choose commands from menus, highlight text, and so on. If you are a new Windows user, we suggest you take a look at *A Quick Course in Windows 3.1*, another book in the *Quick Course* series, which will help you quickly come up to speed.

Microsoft Windows →

To follow the instructions in this book, you must be using a mouse. You can perform many Access functions using the keyboard, but a mouse is required for some tasks. You will find the menus and buttons intuitive and easy to use, and in no time at all, pointing and clicking your way around Access for Windows will seem perfectly natural.

It's time to get started, so let's fire up Windows:

1. With the DOS prompt (C:\>) on your screen, type *win* and press Enter to start Windows.

2. Open the Microsoft Office group window, and double-click the Microsoft Access icon. (If you don't have a Microsoft Office group window, open other group windows until you locate an icon that looks like the one on the right.) The first time you start Access, you see this window, which suggests six ways of learning and getting started with Access:

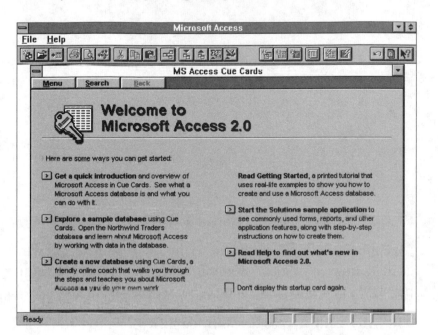

Three of these options involve using Cue Cards, which give steps for carrying out specific Access procedures. One option suggests that you work with one of the sample applications that came with Access. Two options recommend reading parts of the documentation and the Help system to find out how to get going.

3. You don't want to see this screen everytime you start Access, so click the Don't Display This Startup Card Again option in the bottom right corner, and then double-click the Control menu icon—the gray box with the fat hyphen at the left end of the MS Access Cue Cards title bar. Your screen now looks like the one shown at the top of the following page.

Cue Cards

You can display Cue Cards at any point while you are working with Access to get help with basic tasks and procedures. Just click the Cue Cards button (second from the right on the toolbar) to display a window with a list of available topics, and click the topic you want. Access then displays step-by-step instructions. You can leave the window open while you work with your data. To close the window, double-click its Control menu icon.

Control menu   *Title bar*   *Minimize and Restore buttons*

Menu bar
Toolbar

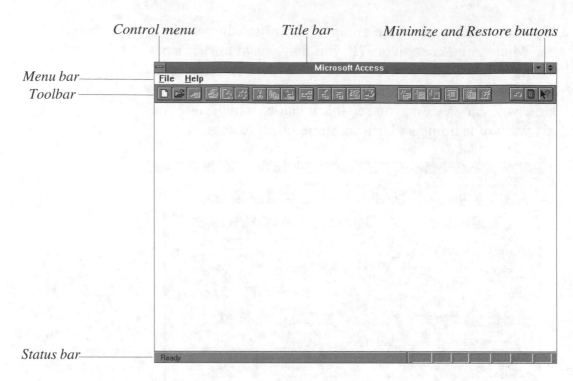

Status bar

Like most Windows applications, the Microsoft Access window includes a title bar, a menu bar, a toolbar, and a status bar. Let's pause to take a quick look at each of them.

The Control menu

The Microsoft Access title bar identifies the program. At its left end is the Control menu icon, which provides commands for manipulating the application and its window and for switching to other applications. At its right end are the Minimize button (the down-pointing arrow), which shrinks the application window to an icon, and the Restore button (the double arrow), which decreases the size of the application window so that you can see other open applications.

The menu bar changes to reflect the menus and commands available for the database component you are working with. Because no database is open at the moment, only the File and Help menus are available. To choose a command from a menu, first click the name of the menu in the menu bar. When the menu drops down, click the name of the command you want. To close a menu without choosing a command, click anywhere outside the menu.

On the menus, some command names are displayed in "gray" letters, indicating that you can't choose those commands at

Shortcut menus

Shortcut menus are context-sensitive menus that group together the commands used most frequently with a specific type of object, such as a field or a window element. You display the shortcut menu by pointing to the object and clicking the right mouse button. You can then choose a command from the menu in the usual way.

this time, and some command names have an arrowhead next to them, indicating that choosing the command will display a submenu. You choose a submenu command the same way you choose a regular command.

Submenus

Some command names are followed by an ellipsis (...), indicating that you must supply more information in a dialog box before Access can carry out the command. You sometimes give the necessary information by typing in an edit box. At other times, you might select options from list boxes or from groups of check boxes and option buttons. You'll use many types of dialog boxes as you work your way through this book, and you'll see how easy they are to work with.

Dialog boxes

The toolbar is a row of buttons that quickly access the most commonly used menu commands. Access displays a different toolbar depending on the database component you are working with. Currently, you see the Database toolbar with all but two buttons dimmed to indicate that they are unavailable. To avoid confusion, a feature called *ToolTips* helps you determine the functions of each button. When you point to a button, ToolTips displays a pop-up box with the button's name and provides a brief description of the button's function at the right end of the status bar.

ToolTips

The status bar at the bottom of your screen displays messages and gives helpful information.

Now that you're familiar with the screen's general layout, let's discuss the concept of a database.

What Is a Database?

The most basic component of an Access database is a *table*— a collection of information arranged in *rows* and *columns*. A database can consist of several tables of related data. For example, a client database might assign clients a number and list their names and addresses in one table and then list their numbers and credit references in another. Still another table might summarize account transactions for the last three years by client number. All the tables contain information about the clients, but each table has different information that is related by the client number. All the information could be kept in just

Custom toolbars

Choosing toolbars from the File menu opens a dialog box that lists all the available toolbars. You can display as many of the toolbars in the current window as you like, by clicking the toolbars' names and then clicking the Show button. Clicking the Customize button opens another dialog box where you can select buttons and drag them to a displayed toolbar. Clicking the Reset button in the Toolbars dialog box returns a customized toolbar to its original configuration.

one table, but if only a few clients have active accounts, the part of the table devoted to account transactions would have only a few entries. It's more efficient to break the database into separate but related tables.

Tables are the basic building blocks of a database. In addition to tables, a database can include queries, forms, reports, and other components, all of which allow you to view and manipulate your database information in a variety of ways. Before you create your first table, let's take a look at one that came with Access. Follow these steps:

Opening existing tables

1. Click the Open Database button on the toolbar. Access displays this dialog box:

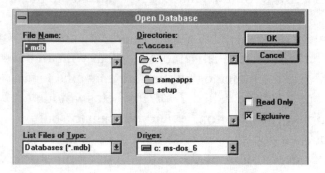

2. In the Directories list, double-click the SAMPAPPS (for *sample applications*) folder icon to display a list of files stored in that directory.

3. In the File Name list, double-click NWIND.MDB to display this dialog box, which allows you to select the component of the NWIND database that you want to view:

4. In the list of tables, click Customers, and then click the Open button. Access opens the sample Customers database in a Table window like the one shown here:

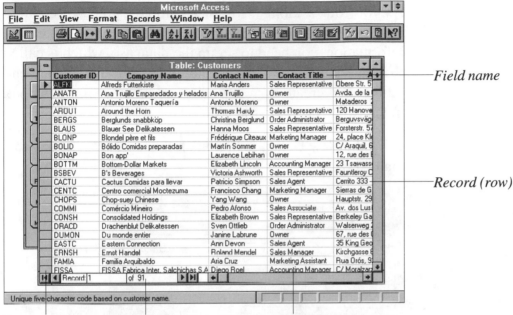

As you can see, a different toolbar is now displayed. The window's title bar identifies the contents of the window as a table and gives its name. The table itself consists of rows of information arranged under column headings, called *field names*, that describe the type of information stored in each column. Each item of information is a *field value*, and each row of items is a *record*. For example, in the Customers table, each company name is a field value, and the record for each customer consists of one row of field values.

Field names and
field values

Records

Now let's close the table so that we can start building our own sample database:

1. Double-click the Table window's Control menu icon, or click it once to display the Control menu and then choose Close. (Be careful not to double-click the Control menu icon at the left end of the Microsoft Access title bar. If you do, you will quit Access and return to the Program Manager window.)

Closing tables

2. Double-click the Control menu icon at the left end of the Database window's title bar to close the window.

Setting Up a Database

As you follow along with our examples, you will create a database for a roofing contractor. Before you can enter any information, you need to set up the database, which is called Roofs. Access will store all the tables, queries, forms, and reports you create as you work your way through this book in the Roofs database file. Follow these steps:

Creating the Roofs database

1. Click the New Database button on the toolbar to display this dialog box:

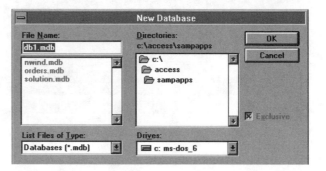

2. Type *roofs* in the File Name edit box, and press Enter or click OK. Access displays this Database window:

Down the left side of the window are buttons for each type of database component. Clicking one of these buttons displays in the box to the right a list of the existing components for that type. Because this is a new database, the Table option is selected, and the box is empty.

Creating a Table

You can now create your first table, which will be used to store employee information. Follow these steps:

1. In the Database window, click New. Access opens this dialog box, in which you specify whether you want the Access Table Wizards to help you set up the new table or whether you prefer to do the setup work yourself:

2. Click Table Wizards to display the first of a series of dialog boxes that lead you through the steps of creating your table's field structure:

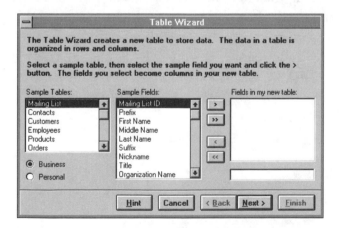

Using Table Wizards to create a table

Wizards

The Access Wizards are tools that walk you through the process of creating standard Access components, such as tables, forms, and reports. You don't have to use the Wizards, but when you are first learning Access, they are a great way to quickly produce a table, form or report. If you make a wrong selection while using one of the Wizards, simply click the Back button to retrace your steps, correct your mistake, and click Next to move forward again.

3. In the Sample Tables list, click Employees. The Sample Fields list changes to reflect the kind of information usually stored in an employee database, with Employee ID selected.

4. Click the > button to add the EmployeeID field name to the Fields In My New Table list.

5. Add the SocialSecurityNumber, FirstName, LastName, Address, City, PostalCode (ZIP code), HomePhone, and DateHired field names to the Fields In My New Table list by clicking each name and then clicking the > button. Then click the Next button to display the next wizard dialog box:

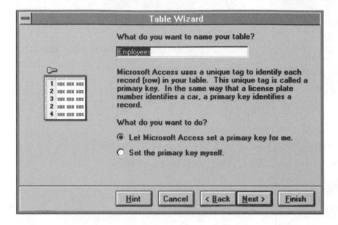

6. The name Access suggests for this database—Employees—is pretty logical, so don't change the entry in the edit box. However, you don't want Access to set the *primary key*, which is a field that distinguishes one record from another. When you enter field values in the table, no two entries in this field can be the same. In keyed tables, if you try to enter the same field value in two records, Access displays an error message and won't let you move to a new record until you change one of the duplicates. Click the Set The Primary Key Myself option, and then click Next. The next wizard dialog box appears:

Primary key

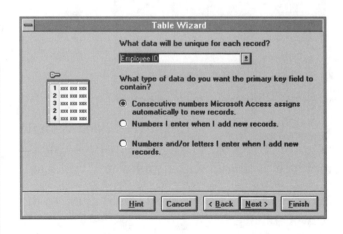

Allowing Access to create the primary key

If you allow Access to create the primary key, Access inserts a Counter field as the first field of the table, designates that field as the primary key, and automatically enters a consecutive number as that field's value for each record.

7. Because you want to set up the primary key yourself, you must now tell Access which field you want to use and what type of data that field will contain. You do want to use the default Employee ID as the primary key, but instead of allowing Access to enter consecutive numbers as the primary key, you want to enter the numbers yourself. Click the second option button, and then click Next. The final Wizard dialog box appears:

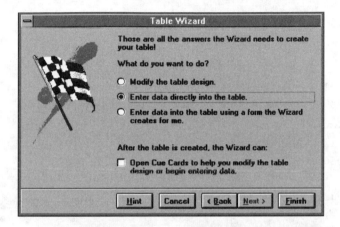

8. Click the Finish button to indicate that you want to enter data directly in the table. Access displays this Table window:

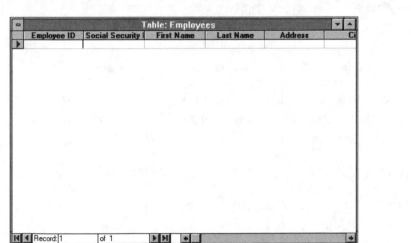

The Table window

Entering Records

Each record in the Employees table will contain information about one employee. In Access, you can enter and edit records either directly in the table or in a form, which displays one record at a time. We'll look at both methods in this section.

Ready-made business and personal tables

The first Table Wizard dialog box provides Business and Personal options, with Business selected by default. If you click the Personal option, Access displays a list of tables you can create for personal use.

Entering Records in a Table

Datasheet view

To enter records in a table, you need to display the table in Datasheet view. Because you told the Table Wizards that you wanted to enter data directly in the table, Access automatically switched the new table to Datasheet view. An insertion point sits blinking in the Employee ID field, ready for you to enter the first item of information, and an arrowhead in the record selector at the left end of the row indicates that the record is ready to receive data.

1. Type *2* as the first employee number. The arrowhead in the row selector changes to a pencil, indicating that the data in the record has been changed but not yet saved. (Access has added a second record with an asterisk in its row selector, indicating that the record is empty.) Press Enter to move the insertion point to the next field.

2. Enter these field values in the first record, pressing Enter to move from field to field:

Field	Record 1
Social Security Number	796294473 (Access inserts the hyphens)
First Name	Carol
Last Name	Talbot
Address	1109 Emerson Way
City	Lakewood
Postal Code	11403 (Access adds a hyphen)

Data entry shortcuts

While you are entering or editing a field, pressing Ctrl+Z undoes your typing, pressing Esc once clears all changes to the field, and pressing Esc twice clears changes to the record. If the preceding field contains the data you want in the current field, pressing Ctrl+' copies the data. Pressing Ctrl+Alt+Spacebar restores the field's default value. Pressing F2 switches between editing and navigational modes.

3. Click the Home Phone field, click an insertion point to the right of the area code's open parenthesis, and press the Right Arrow key three times. Then type *3347625*, and press Enter.

4. In the Date Hired field, type *08/27/79*, and press Enter.

Don't worry that the data in the Address field doesn't fit within its column. On page 18, we show you how to adjust the width of fields so that you can see all the information in the table on one screen.

5. Enter the data for records 2 through 5, remembering to use the Right Arrow key to skip over the area code in the Home Phone field:

Field	Record 2	Record 3	Record 4	Record 5
Employee ID	19	27	29	33
Social Security Number	228129111	854722249	934218635	583021253
First Name	Ron	Fred	James	Lance
Last Name	Westerman	Anderson	Murray	Bright
Address	1419 Ivy Drive	943 Spruce Circle	7921 Port Avenue	148 Center St, #B211
City	Pinedale	Lakewood	Lakewood	Pinedale
Postal Code	11412	11403	11403	11412
Home Phone	3351326	8328779	8345934	3346683
Date Hired	09/08/85	02/14/89	03/22/91	06/23/91

The Employees table now looks like this:

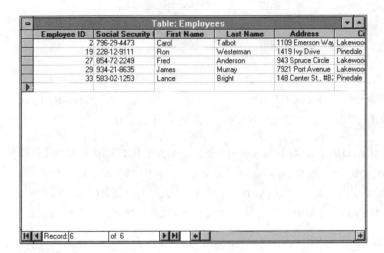

Entering Records in a Form

Instead of entering your information in a table, you can enter it in a *form*. The simplest type of form shows one record at a time with the field names one under the other on the left side and the corresponding field values on the right side. (If this default format doesn't meet your needs, you can design your own format; see Chapter 4 for information about custom forms.) To display the form for the Employee table and see how easy it is to enter records in a form, follow the steps on the next page.

Fast navigation

When entering and editing data, using the keyboard to move around a window is often faster than using the mouse. You can easily navigate using the Arrow, Tab, Home, End, Page Up, and Page Down keys.

1. Click the AutoForm button on the toolbar to display the form shown here (resize the window if necessary—see page 18):

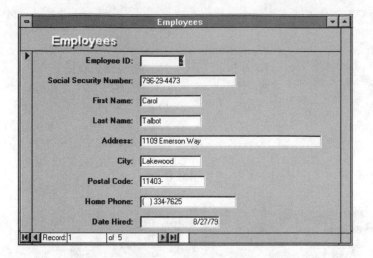

Displaying the next record

2. Click the right-pointing arrowhead next to the record indicator—the Next Record button—at the bottom of the window to display the information for Ron Westerman.

Displaying the last record

Adding records

3. Click the right-pointing arrowhead with the bar—the Last Record button—to move to the last record in the table, and then click the Next Record button to display a blank record. Or simply click the New Record button on the toolbar.

4. Use the information in the following table to enter the record for the sixth employee. After typing the last field value, press Enter to display a new blank record, type the data for the seventh employee, and press Enter.

Field	Record 6	Record 7
Employee ID	34	35
Social Security Number	477116309	722522624
First Name	Richard	Linda
Last Name	Talbot	Gardner
Address	1109 Emerson Way	8841 Market Street
City	Lakewood	Lakewood
Postal Code	11403	11403
Home Phone	3347625	3346754
Date Hired	06/23/91	05/02/92

Now that you have entered these records in the table, you can tell Access to prevent any further editing of the records so that you don't inadvertently change or delete any of them. Here are the steps:

1. Choose Allow Editing from the Records menu to turn off the editing option.

Preventing further editing

2. Try to make changes to the data.

The Employees table is complete for now, and you can view the records in either Form view or Datasheet view. Here's how to switch back and forth:

1. Click the Datasheet View button on the toolbar. Instead of the form, you now see the table.

Switching to Datasheet view

2. Click the Form View button on the toolbar to switch back to the form.

Switching to Form view

As long as either the table or the form is open, you can click these buttons to switch between the two views.

When you are working with a table that requires constant updating, you can save the form so that it is available whenever you need it. For now, you want to close the form without saving it so that you can see what the Employees table looks like. Follow these steps:

1. Double-click the Form window's Control menu icon, and click No when Access asks whether you want to save the changes to the form.

Closing forms

Updating the Table

The Employees table is now visible, but the records you entered via the form are not displayed. You need to update the table, like this:

1. Click the Show All Records button on the toolbar. Access updates the table to show the last two records.

Moving Around the Table

You can move around the table using either the mouse or the keyboard. Like most Windows programs, Access automatically adds scroll bars along the bottom and right sides of the window if the table is too wide or too tall to be displayed in its entirety. You can click the scroll arrows to scroll to the left or right one field at a time or up or down one record at a time. Click on either side of the scroll box to scroll one screenful of records at a time.

Scrolling

As well as using the scroll bars, you can click the buttons on either side of the record indicator at the bottom of the window. The Previous Record and Next Record buttons move you through the table one record at a time, and the First Record and Last Record buttons move you to the first or last record in the table.

Using the navigation buttons

The keyboard is often a faster way to move around the table. Here's a list of the keys you can use:

Using the keyboard

Key	Moves
Tab	Horizontally one field at a time.
Right and Left Arrows	When a field is highlighted, horizontally one field at a time; otherwise, moves the insertion point one character at a time.
Up and Down Arrows	Vertically one field at a time.
Home	To the first field in the current record.
End	To the last field in the current record.
Ctrl+Home	To the first field in the first record.
Ctrl+End	To the last field in the last record.
Page Down	Down one screenful of records.
Page Up	Up one screenful of records.
Ctrl+Page Down	To the right one screenful of fields.
Ctrl+Page Up	To the left one screenful of fields.

Practice moving around the Employees table using the mouse and keyboard. Knowing the navigational methods is useful because you can then select the method most appropriate for a particular situation. As you can imagine, the ability to jump to the beginning or end of a table and to move through records a screenful at a time is especially useful with tables that contain thousands of records.

Finding Specific Records

You will often need to find either a particular record in a table or all the records that have something in common, so Access provides an easy way to locate records. As a demonstration, let's search the Employees table for a record with Talbot in the Last Name field:

1. Select the Last Name field of any record by pointing to the left of the field value and, when the pointer changes to a hollow right-pointing arrow, clicking to highlight the field.

2. Click the Find button on the toolbar to display the Find dialog box shown here:

3. Point to the Find dialog box's title bar, hold down the mouse button, and drag the dialog box downward so that you can see the table's records.

Moving dialog boxes

4. Type *Talbot* in the Find What edit box, and then click the Find First button. Access highlights the first field value that matches your specification.

Finding the first record

5. Suppose this is not the employee record you need to examine. Click the Find Next button in the dialog box to display the next record with Talbot in the Last Name field.

Finding subsequent records

6. Click the Close button to close the dialog box.

When dealing with a very large table, you can temporarily focus on a subset of the records in the table by using *filters*. Clicking the Edit Filter/Sort button on the toolbar displays a Filter window in which you can set up the criteria that define the subset. Clicking the Apply Filter/Sort button applies the filter to the records and displays the subset. Filters are closely related to *queries*, which you'll learn about in Chapter 3.

Changing the Table's Appearance

Like most people, you're probably more interested in using database tables to get the information you need than in making your data look fancy, but sometimes a little customization can actually make tables easier to work with. This type of customization changes the way the table looks but doesn't alter its data.

Sizing Tables and Fields

You can often squeeze more information on the screen by enlarging the table window or by adjusting the sizes of fields. Perhaps you've noticed that as you move your mouse around the screen, the pointer sometimes changes shape. On the frame of a window, on the gridlines between the field names, and on the dividing lines between the row selectors, the pointer changes to various kinds of double-headed arrows. While the pointer has this shape, you can resize the table window or the fields.

To resize the window, simply point to its frame and use the double-headed arrow to move that frame in or out to decrease or increase the window's size.

Resizing fields is equally simple, as you'll see if you follow these steps:

Changing field width with the mouse

1. Move the pointer to the gridline between the Address and City field names.

2. When the pointer changes to a double-headed arrow, hold down the left mouse button, and drag to the right. As you drag, the width of the Address field grows. When you think the entire field name will be visible, release the mouse button.

Changing field height with the mouse

3. Point to the dividing line between the first and second row selectors, and then drag downward to increase the heights of all the fields in all the records.

Here's another way to change the widths of fields:

1. Scroll the table until the last four fields are visible. Move the pointer to the City field name, and when the pointer changes to a downward-pointing arrow, click to select that field in all records. Then move the pointer to the Date Hired field name,

hold down the Shift key, and click to add the Postal Code, Home Phone, and Date Hired fields to the selection.

2. Choose Column Width from the Format menu to display this dialog box:

Using the Column Width dialog box

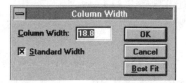

3. Type *15*, and press Enter to change the widths of all four fields at the same time.

The Format menu also includes a Row Height command that allows you to set the heights of the rows precisely. Here's how to restore the original heights of the rows:

1. Choose Row Height from the Format menu to display this dialog box:

Using the Row Height dialog box

2. Click the Standard Height check box, and then click OK.

You might want to take some time to practice resizing the Employees table's fields; for example, try shrinking the fields enough to see all of them at one time.

Moving Fields

By default, the fields are displayed in the order in which you entered them when you designed the table. You can change the field order by selecting a field's column and dragging it to a new position. For example, if you want to look up an employee's phone number, it might be useful to see the Home Phone field next to the employee names. Follow the steps on the next page to move the Home Phone field.

Freezing fields

To freeze a single field in position while scrolling other fields, click anywhere in the field, and then choose Freeze Columns from the Format menu. The field moves to the left to become the first column in the table. You can then scroll the remaining fields. To freeze a set of fields, click the first field in the set, hold down Shift, click the last field, and then choose Freeze Columns. Choose Unfreeze All Columns to remove the freeze.

1. Scroll the Table window, and click the Home Phone field name to select the entire column.

2. Point to the Home Phone field name, hold down the left mouse button, and drag the field to the left. As you move the field, Access highlights the divider lines between columns to indicate the new position of the Home Phone field.

3. When the divider line to the right of the Last Name field is highlighted, release the mouse button. As you can see here, the Home Phone field moves to its new position:

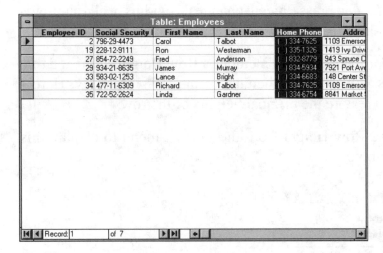

4. For more practice, move the Home Phone field back to its original position between the Postal Code and Date Hired fields.

   Moving fields in Datasheet view does not affect the data or change the basic structure of the table.

Hiding and Unhiding Fields

In addition to moving fields, you can choose not to display specific fields. For example, you might want to hide employees' social security numbers and hire dates. Follow the steps below to hide these fields:

Hiding fields

1. Click the Social Security Number field name to select the column.

2. Choose Hide Columns from the Format menu. You can no longer see the Social Security Number column.

3. Repeat steps 1 and 2 for the Date Hired column.

The Social Security Number and Date Hired fields still exist in the table; they are just not visible right now. Here's how to make them visible again:

1. Choose Show Columns from the Format menu to display this dialog box:

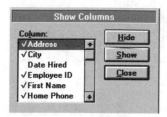

Notice that you can also hide columns using the Hide button in this dialog box.

2. Click the Date Hired field name to select it, and then click the Show Button.

3. Scroll to the Social Security Number field name, click Show, and then click Close to close the dialog box.

Other Customizable Options

You can customize several parts of the Access window, as well as control other table functions and properties, by choosing the Options command from the View menu. We won't make any changes now, but we will take a look at the dialog box that Access displays when we choose this command.

1. Choose Options from the View menu to display the dialog box shown here:

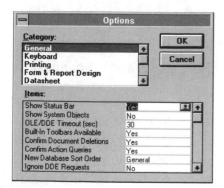

Optional gridlines

The gridlines that separate the columns and rows in an Access table are optional. You can remove them by choosing the Gridlines command from the Format menu to toggle them off.

As you can see, the Options dialog box has two lists: the Category list at the top and the Items list below. Clicking a category causes a different list of items to be displayed. Clicking the edit box of some items displays an arrow, and clicking the arrow displays a list of the options available for that item.

2. For now, take a careful look at the items available for each category so that as you use Access you'll know where to look if you want to change an option. Then click Cancel to close the dialog box.

Changing the Font

One way to change the look of a table is to change the font used for the field values. You may have noticed in the Options dialog box that the Datasheet category has several items related to fonts. You can also change the font, size, and style of the entire table by using menu commands. Follow these steps:

1. Choose Font from the Format menu to display the Font dialog box shown here (your fonts may be different):

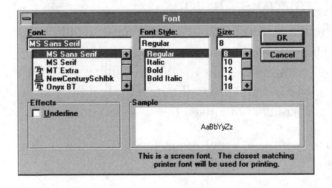

Adding bold ──────────────→ 2. In the Font Style section, click Bold.

3. Click OK to see the result. All the field values in the table are now bold. (You cannot use the Font command to change only part of the table.)

4. You can easily change the font and font size and draw lines under field values to make them stand out. Go ahead and experiment with some of the font options, returning the table to its original settings—MS Sans Serif, Regular, and 8, with no underline—when you've finished.

Changing the Table's Structure

You've seen how to make cosmetic changes that affect the way your database table looks on the screen. Now let's explore ways you can affect the underlying structure of the table. When you used the Table Wizards to set up the Employees table, Access made a number of decisions about the table's basic design. But those decisions are not cast in stone. Let's examine Access's default table structure and see how to change it:

1. Click the Design View button on the toolbar. Access displays the structure of your table in this window:

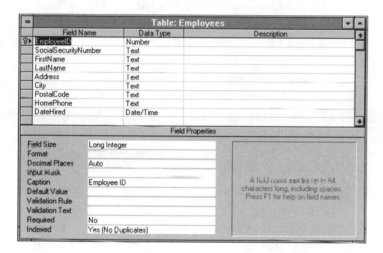

As you can see, the window is divided into two sections. The top half lists the table's field names (with no spaces) and their data type. (Specifying the data type determines what kind of information you can put in the field and how Access can work with the information.) The bottom half lists the properties assigned to the field selected in the top half.

2. Press Enter to move to the Data Type column for the EmployeeID field, and display a list of the available data types by clicking the arrow that appears. You may not want to spend much time learning about all the Access data types now, but for future reference we'll group them in a table, shown on the next page, so that you can find them when you are specifying the field types for your own database tables.

Access data types

Data Type	Description
Text	General purpose data. Can contain letters, numbers, and other characters such as &, %, =, and ?. Cannot have a null value. Can have up to 255 characters; (the default is 50).
Memo	Similar to text, except that size limit is 64,000 bytes instead of 255 characters. Cannot be indexed. (See page 142 for more information.)
Number	Includes these formats: *Byte*: Whole numbers between 0 and 255. *Integer*: Whole numbers between $-32,767$ and $32,768$. *Long Integer*: Whole numbers between $-2,147,483,647$ and $2,147,483,648$. *Single*: Single-precision floating-point numbers between $-3.402823E38$ and $3.402823E38$. *Double*: Double-precision floating-point numbers between $-1.79769313486232E308$ and $1.79769313486232E308$.
Date/Time	Valid dates are from January 1, 100 to December 31, 9999, including leap years. Can show dates, times, or both. Can have a variety of formats. (See page 26 for more information.)
Currency	Number data formatted with up to 4 digits to the right of the decimal point and up to 15 to the left. Currency data typically shows negative values in red and has money formatting. Can also be used for fixed-point calculations on number data.
Counter	A sequential number automatically assigned by Access to each new record in the table. Can be used as the primary key field for tables in which none of the fields have a unique set of values. Cannot be indexed.
Yes/No	Use for data that has only two possible values, such as yes/no or on/off.
OLE Object	Can hold graphics or other data created with Windows OLE-supporting applications. (OLE stands for *object linking and embedding*.) Cannot be indexed. (See page 44 for more information.)

Restructure warning

When restructuring a table, bear in mind that some data types cannot be converted to other types without loss of data. Adding a new primary key may result in key violations, and reducing field sizes may result in a loss of data. If you attempt a restructure that will result in corrupted or lost data, Access advises you of the problem and gives you the choice of proceeding or canceling the restructure.

3. Click Number to close the Data Type list without changing its setting, and press Enter to move to the Description column.

Adding field descriptions

4. Type *Unique 3-character number identifies each employee.* When the table is displayed and this field is selected, this description will appear in the status bar.

Using Field Properties

Below the table grid that defines the fields for the table is the Field Properties section, where you can refine your field definitions. You will use some of these properties frequently, others rarely. In this section, we'll explore the more common properties.

Setting the Field Size

You can set a field size for both the text and number data types. For text fields, the size indicates the maximum number of characters you can enter in the field. Up to 255 characters are allowed. If you try to enter, paste, or import a field value that is longer than the specified size, Access truncates the data.

Text field size

Follow these steps to set the size of the text fields of the Employees table:

1. Click anywhere in the SocialSecurityNumber field in the table grid to display the default properties for that field in the Field Properties section.

2. Double-click *30* in the Field Size edit box to select it, and type *11* to indicate that the field can have up to eleven characters.

3. Repeat steps 1 and 2 to assign the following field sizes:

Field	Size	Field	Size
FirstName	10	City	12
LastName	12	PostalCode	10
Address	25	HomePhone	20

The Field Size property for number fields is different from that of text fields. The size of a number field is determined by the complexity of the format selected. (See the table on the facing page for more information.)

Number field size

Follow these steps to set the size of the table's number fields:

Changing number field size

1. Click anywhere in the EmployeeID field, and then click the Field Size edit box in the Field Properties section.

2. Click the arrow to see a list of available sizes. You don't think the company will ever employ more than 255 employees, so select Byte.

Setting the Format

The Format property lets you specify how the characters entered in a field are to be displayed on the screen. The type of formatting you can perform varies depending on the data type. For example, you can select one of several predefined formats for date/time fields, like this:

Selecting a predefined format

1. Click anywhere in the DateHired field, and then click the Format edit box in the Field Properties section.

2. Click the arrow to see a list of predefined formats, and select Medium Date. The dates in the table will now be displayed in dd-mmm-yy format.

In addition to selecting predefined formats, for some data types you can specify custom formats. Follow these steps to tell Access to always display three digits in the EmployeeID field:

Specifying a custom format

1. Click anywhere in the EmployeeID field, and then click the Format edit box.

2. Type *000* to tell Access to enter three digits, using zeros unless you enter something else. Now if you enter an EmployeeID of *36*, Access will display the entry as *036*.

Specifying the Input Mask

Formats aren't the only way to control the display of data. You can also specify an *input mask*, or character pattern, that not only determines how your data looks on the screen but also what kind of data can be entered in a particular field. Because you used the Table Wizard to set up the Employees table, Access has already specified input masks for some fields. Let's take a look at a few of these input masks and make any necessary changes:

1. Click anywhere in the SocialSecurityNumber field. The entry in the Input Mask edit box is *000\-00\-0000*. The zeros are placeholders for digits that you must enter, and the back-slashes indicate that the hyphens are literal characters that Access will insert for you.

2. Click the PostalCode field in the table grid. The entry in the Input Mask edit box changes to *00000\-9999*. Again, the zeros are placeholders for digits you must enter. The nines are placeholders for an optional four-digit ZIP code extension. Access enters the hyphen whether or not you enter this extension.

3. Click an insertion point after the last 9, and press Backspace six times to delete all but the five zeros. Now Access will accept only five digits in this field.

Now let's adjust an input mask with some help from Access:

1. Click the HomePhone field in the table grid. The entry in the Input Mask edit box changes to *!\(999") "000\-0000*.

2. Click the Input Mask edit box, and then click the Build button—the button with three asterisks to the right of the edit box. Click Yes when Access tells you it must save the table before proceeding, and when another message box warns you that the changes you have made to the field sizes of the table might result in a loss of data, click OK to proceed. Access then displays this Input Mask Wizard dialog box:

Input Mask Wizard

3. Click Next to accept the default Phone Number option and display the dialog box shown on the following page.

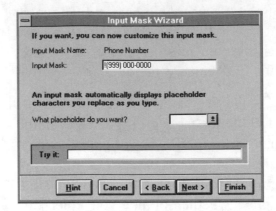

The 9s in the parentheses indicate that a three-digit area code is optional, whereas the seven-digit phone number is required.

4. All the employees live in the same area code, so you want to enter only the seven-digit phone number without having to skip the area code. In the Input Mask edit box, click to the left of the first 0, and then press the Backspace key to delete *!(999)* and the extra space.

5. Click the arrow to the right of the placeholder edit box, and select the underscore from the drop-down list.

Trying out the mask

6. Now click at the left end of the Try It edit box, and type your phone number. Then backspace over the last four digits, and try typing *abcd*. Access won't accept letters in the entry because the zeros in the input mask require the entry of digits.

7. Press Esc to clear the Try It entry, and click the Next button to display this dialog box:

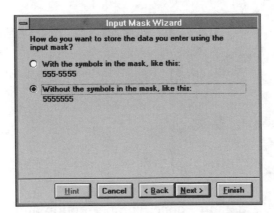

8. Click Finish to accept the default setting in the last Wizard dialog box and return to the table window.

Here's a list of some common characters used in the Input Mask edit box, together with what they mean to Access:

Input mask characters

Character	Access's Action
L	Require a letter.
?	Allow any letter; if no letter is entered, leave blank.
&	Allow any character.
0	Require a digit; if no digit is entered, insert 0.
#	Allow any digit; if no digit is entered, leave blank.
<	Convert all following characters to lowercase.
>	Convert all following characters to uppercase.
\	Insert the following character as entered.

Let's use some of these characters to enter a couple of new input masks:

1. Click the FirstName field in the table grid, and in the Input Mask edit box, type *>L<?????????* (with nine question marks) to tell Access to allow up to ten letters and to ensure that the first letter is capitalized.

2. Click the LastName field, and enter *>L<???????????* (with eleven question marks) as the input mask.

Assigning a Caption

The Caption property enables you to substitute text for the field name when you display the table. The caption may simply repeat the field name with spaces added for readability, or it may display something different. Let's change a few of the captions specified by the Table Wizards when you created the table:

1. Click anywhere in the EmployeeID field to display its properties in the Field Properties section.

2. Click an insertion point to the right of the *p* in *Employee* in the Caption edit box, hold down the Shift key, and press the End key to highlight all but *Emp*. Then type #.

Input mask sections

The Input Mask edit box displays three items of information about the input mask, separated by semicolons. The first item is the mask itself; the second item indicates whether literal characters are stored with the mask (1 or blank specifies No, and 0 specifies Yes); and the third item indicates the placeholder character.

3. Repeat steps 1 and 2 to change the following captions:

Social Security Number to SS#
Postal Code to Zip
HomePhone to Phone#
Date Hired to First Day

When you display the table, the new captions will be displayed as field names, above each column of information.

Setting a Default Value

The Default Value property lets you specify a field value that Access is to enter in the table automatically. Because the sample roofing company is small and most of the employees live in the same city, you can use this property for both the City and PostalCode fields to speed up data entry. Follow these steps:

1. Click anywhere in the City field to display that field's properties in the Field Properties section.

2. In the Default Value edit box, click to display an insertion point, and then type *Lakewood* as the default city name.

3. Repeat steps 1 and 2 for the PostalCode field, specifying *11403* as the default value.

Now every record you enter in the new database table will have Lakewood as its City field value and 11403 as its PostalCode field value, unless you replace them with something else.

Requiring Entries

If you leave the table's field structure as it is, it would be possible to create incomplete employee records. To ensure that key information is always entered, you can specify that a field must have an entry. Try this:

1. Click the EmployeeID field, click the Required edit box, click the arrow, and then click Yes.

2. Repeat step 1 for all the other fields.

Defining Indexes

When you made the EmployeeID field the primary key for the table, Access changed the Indexed field property to Yes

(No Duplicates), meaning that the field is indexed and no duplicate values will be allowed. Only text, number, currency, and date/time fields can be indexed. When a field is indexed, Access can process queries, searches, and sorts based on the field more quickly. (If a few values will be repeated often in a field, as is the case with the City and PostalCode fields, then indexing the field will not save much processing time.) Data entry and editing may be slower with indexed fields because Access must maintain the index as well as the table.

The three remaining properties in the Field Properties section enable you to set up systems for checking the validity of the data you enter in your tables. The Validation Rule and Validation Text properties are discussed in more detail on page 58. You will rarely need to use the Allow Zero Length property (available for text fields), so we don't set it for any of the fields in this table.

Other properties

Switching Back to the Table

Now let's return to the table to see the effects of our changes:

1. Click the Datasheet View button on the toolbar. Access tells you it must save the table before it can switch views.

2. Click OK. When Access asks whether you want to test the data in the table against the new properties, click Yes. Access then displays the Table window.

3. Increase the table's size and decrease the width of the fields so that you can see all the employee data at once, like this:

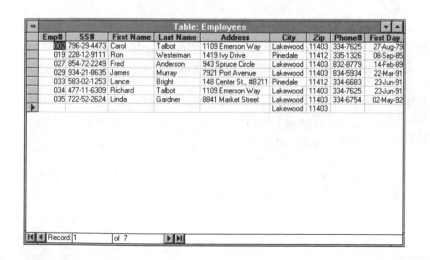

Data integrity

Always stop and think before changing the field sizes and input masks for your data. Such changes can result in data losses that will seriously affect the usability of some fields. For example, if you had entered area codes in the HomePhone field, changing the input mask might have resulted in the last three digits of the employees' phone numbers being chopped off.

The table reflects all the visual changes you made to its structure. The Emp# field displays three digits, and *Lakewood* and *11403* have been entered by default in the blank record at the bottom of the table. Let's add one more employee to try everything out:

4. Click the Emp# field of the blank record at the bottom of the table, type *38*, and press Enter. Access enters *038* in the field.

5. Enter the following information in the indicated fields (press Enter to skip over the City and Zip fields):

Field	Record 8
SS#	241214972
First Name	jonathan
Last Name	bray
Address	5941 Hilltop Road
Phone#	3340180
First Day	06/17/92

As you enter the field values, notice the effect of the field properties specified as part of the table's structure.

Getting Help

This has been a whistle-stop tour of Access tables, and you might not remember everything we've covered. If you forget how to carry out a particular task, help is never far away. You've already seen how the ToolTips feature can jog your memory about the functions of the toolbar buttons. Access also offers several other ways to get information.

You can get immediate help with the task at hand by using the Help button on the toolbar. For example, here's how to get information about toolbar buttons and menu commands:

1. Click the Help button, move the question-mark pointer to the Find button on the toolbar, and click. Access displays a Help window with information about the Find button.

2. Double-click the Control menu icon at the left end of the Help window's title bar to close the window.

3. Now click the Help button, click *Format* on the menu bar with the question-mark pointer, and then click the Hide Columns command. Access displays information about the command.

When a dialog box is open on your screen, you can display information about its options by pressing the F1 key.

If you need information about an Access procedure or how to accomplish a particular task, you can use the commands on the Help menu. Choosing Contents and clicking any of the options in the Help Contents window takes you to topic lists that enable you to find the information you need. Clicking a topic with dotted underscores displays a pop-up definition, and clicking a topic with solid underscores takes you to related information. Choosing Search from the Help menu displays a dialog box in which you enter the procedure or task you want information about. You can then narrow your search by selecting a specific topic from a list.

It's worth taking a little time to explore the Access Help system. You might want to experiment with the various methods of getting assistance as you work your way through this book.

Ending an Access Session

Well, that's a lot of work for one chapter, and you're probably ready for a break. When you finish working with Access, all you have to do is quit. You don't need to worry about saving the information in open database tables; Access updates the table files one record at a time as you enter or edit records. If you make any changes to the properties of a table (the way the table is displayed on the screen, not the table's structure or its records), Access asks whether you want to save those changes before it closes the table. Let's quit Access now:

Automatic saving

1. Quit Access by double-clicking the program's Control menu icon. (You can also choose Exit from the File menu.)

Quitting Access

2. If Access asks whether you want to save your layout changes, click Yes.

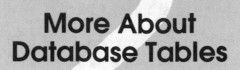

More About
Database Tables

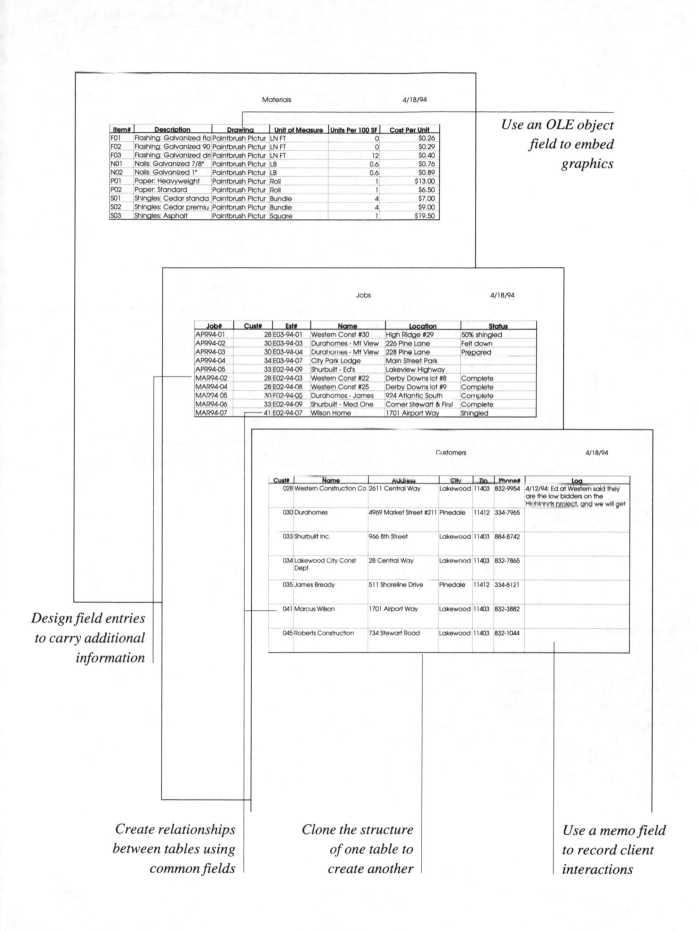

Materials   4/18/94

Item#	Description	Drawing	Unit of Measure	Units Per 100 SF	Cost Per Unit
F01	Flashing: Galvanized fla	Paintbrush Pictur	LN FT	0	$0.26
F02	Flashing: Galvanized 90	Paintbrush Pictur	LN FT	0	$0.29
F03	Flashing: Galvanized dri	Paintbrush Pictur	LN FT	12	$0.40
N01	Nails: Galvanized 7/8"	Paintbrush Pictur	LB	0.6	$0.76
N02	Nails: Galvanized 1"	Paintbrush Pictur	LB	0.6	$0.89
P01	Paper: Heavyweight	Paintbrush Pictur	Roll	1	$13.00
P02	Paper: Standard	Paintbrush Pictur	Roll	1	$6.50
S01	Shingles: Cedar standa	Paintbrush Pictur	Bundle	4	$7.00
S02	Shingles: Cedar premiu	Paintbrush Pictur	Bundle	4	$9.00
S03	Shingles: Asphalt	Paintbrush Pictur	Square	1	$19.50

Use an OLE object field to embed graphics

Jobs   4/18/94

Job#	Cust#	Est#	Name	Location	Status
APR94-01	28	E03-94-01	Western Const #30	High Ridge #29	50% shingled
APR94-02	30	E03-94-03	Durahomes - Mt View	226 Pine Lane	Felt down
APR94-03	30	E03-94-04	Durahomes - Mt View	228 Pine Lane	Prepared
APR94-04	34	E03-94-07	City Park Lodge	Main Street Park	
APR94-05	33	E02-94-09	Shurbuilt - Ed's	Lakeview Highway	
MAR94-02	28	E02-94-03	Western Const #22	Derby Downs lot #8	Complete
MAR94-04	28	E02-94-08	Western Const #25	Derby Downs lot #9	Complete
MAR94 05	30	F02-94-05	Durahomes - James	924 Atlantic South	Complete
MAR94-06	33	E02-94-09	Shurbuilt - Med One	Corner Stewart & First	Complete
MAR94-07	41	E02-94-07	Wilson Home	1701 Airport Way	Shingled

Customers   4/18/94

Cust#	Name	Address	City	Zip	Phone#	Log
028	Western Construction Co	2611 Central Way	Lakewood	11403	832-9954	4/12/94: Ed at Western said they are the low bidders on the Highlands project, and we will get
030	Durahomes	4969 Market Street #211	Pinedale	11412	334-7965	
033	Shurbuilt Inc.	966 8th Street	Lakewood	11403	884-8742	
034	Lakewood City Const Dept	28 Central Way	Lakewood	11403	832-7865	
035	James Bready	511 Shoreline Drive	Pinedale	11412	334-8121	
041	Marcus Wilson	1701 Airport Way	Lakewood	11403	832-3882	
045	Roberts Construction	734 Stewart Road	Lakewood	11403	832-1044	

Design field entries to carry additional information

Create relationships between tables using common fields

Clone the structure of one table to create another

Use a memo field to record client interactions

Simple tables like the one we created in Chapter 1 will probably meet many of your needs. However, relational databases like Access enable you to add features that make tables more powerful and to manipulate tables so that you can easily access the information they contain. In this chapter, we look at more ways to work with database tables.

Copying Tables

Suppose you want to experiment with the Employees table but you want to be sure that the original data remains intact in case your experiments don't work as well as you'd like. You can't simply copy the Employees file in File Manager or at the DOS prompt to safeguard the data because Access tables don't exist as separate files; they are part of the database file. Instead, you can copy the table in Access, using the Copy button on the toolbar or the Copy command on the Edit menu. Follow these steps to copy the Employees table:

1. Start Access, click the Open Database button on the toolbar, display the files stored in the SAMPAPPS directory, select ROOFS.MDB, and click OK.

2. With the Employees table selected in the Database window, click the Copy button on the toolbar.

3. Click the Paste button on the toolbar. Access displays the Paste Table As dialog box, which allows you to specify a name for the copy of the table. You can also specify whether you want to copy only the structure of the table (see page 40 for more information about this option), to copy the structure and the data (the default selection), or to append the copied data to the existing data in the table.

4. In the Table Name edit box, type *Empcopy* as the name of the new table, and press Enter. Access creates Empcopy using the structure and data from Employees and lists the new table in the Database window, like this:

Editing buttons

The Cut, Copy, and Paste buttons on the toolbar offer shortcuts for accessing the three most common editing commands. You can cut or copy and paste number, text, or date values within the same table or in other tables. You can also paste in data from other applications. No matter where the data comes from, it must be compatible with the receiving field's data type.

5. Double-click Empcopy to display the table, and enlarge the table window so that you can see more of the data.

Opening the copy

Editing Table Data

If your data were a simple list that didn't change, you could keep it on paper. But data is often dynamic, and you need to be able to delete, insert, and otherwise change records to keep a database current. You already know how to edit the values in individual fields. In the next few pages, we show you different ways of manipulating entire records.

Deleting Records

To delete a record, you simply select the record and choose the Delete command. Follow these steps to delete Fred Anderson's record from the Empcopy table:

1. Select Fred Anderson's record by clicking its record selector, and choose Delete from the Edit menu or press the Delete key. Access displays this dialog box:

2. Click OK. Access deletes the record and updates the table.

Be careful when deleting records. If you make a mistake and delete the wrong record, you can't restore the record by clicking

Turning off confirmation

If you delete or change records on a regular basis, you can disable the confirmation dialog box by choosing Options from the View menu and changing the Confirm Record Changes item in the General category to No. Be careful! If you highlight a record and hit the Delete key, Access will delete it without warning.

an Undo button or choosing Undo from the Edit menu once you've confirmed the deletion.

Copying Records

When you want to update a record in one table to reflect the record in another table, you can use the Copy and Paste buttons or the equivalent commands on the Edit menu as long as the tables' fields are of compatible types. Here's how to copy a record from the Employees table to the Empcopy table:

Copying records from one table to another

1. Click the Database Window button on the toolbar to activate the Database window, select Employees, and click Open.

2. Select Fred Anderson's record, and click the Copy button on the toolbar.

3. Click the Empcopy table's window to activate it, and choose Paste Append from the Edit menu. Access adds Fred Anderson's record to the end of the table.

4. Click the Show All Records button on the toolbar. Access updates the order of records according to their primary key values so that Fred Anderson's record is in Emp# sequence.

5. Double-click the Control menu icon at the left end of the Empcopy table's title bar to close its window.

Field compatibility

If the fields in the source table (the one you are copying from) are in a different order than the fields in the destination table (the one you are pasting into), rearrange the fields in the destination table so that they reflect the order in the source table before copying the record. If the source table has more fields than the destination table, the surplus field will be lost when you paste the record. If the destination table has more fields than the source table, the surplus fields will be blank after you paste the record.

The Paste Errors table

If Access encounters a problem when pasting the record into the destination table, it puts the problem records in a Paste Errors table, which shows up in the list of tables in the Database window. Errors might result from such problems as incompatible data types, violation of a validation rule, a text field value that is longer than the specified size, or a field value that duplicates a value in the primary key field. By scrutinizing the Paste Errors table, you can usually discover the problem and fix it. You can then cut and paste the records from the Paste Errors table into the destination table.

Inserting New Records

Inserting a new record at the end of a table is a simple matter of clicking the blank record designated by the asterisk and entering your data. Here's how to insert a new record in a specific place in a table:

1. Select the record above which you want to insert the new record—in this case, select Jonathan Bray's record.

Inserting a blank record

2. Choose Data Entry from the Records menu. Access displays a single record in which you enter your data:

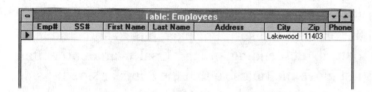

Enter the following data for this record:

Field	Record 9
Emp#	37
SS#	455829921
First Name	Jeffrey
Last Name	Davis
Address	1171 Simpson Heights
City	(Press Enter)
Zip	(Press Enter)
Phone#	3349297
First Day	6/12/92

You can press Enter if you want to add another record.

3. Click the Show All Records button on the toolbar to see the table with your new record.

Note that in a keyed table, Access automatically orders the records based on the values in the primary key field, so inserting records out of order is a waste of time.

Record order

Sorting Records

The Employees table is short enough that you can view all its records on the screen at one time. But you may work with tables, such as mailing lists, that contain several hundred or even several thousand records. In those tables, one way to easily locate a specific record or set of records is to sort the table on a particular field. (We briefly mentioned two other ways, using the Find dialog box and using filters, on page 17. Chapter 3 covers yet another method, using queries.)

To sort the records of a table in Datasheet view, select the column you want to sort on. (You cannot sort on a memo or OLE object field.) Then click the Sort Ascending button on the toolbar to sort starting with A or the lowest digit, or click the Sort Descending button to sort starting with Z or the highest digit. To sort the records on more than one column, you must first arrange the columns so that they appear in the table in the order of the sort. For example, to sort a table of invoice data in descending order of sales amount within region, first move the fields so that they appear side-by-side with the region column to the left of the sales amount column (see page 19). Then select the two columns, and click the Sort Descending button. Access sorts the records first into descending order by region and then into descending order by sales amount within each region.

Cloning Tables

Databases often consist of several tables with the same general characteristics. For example, the database for the roofing company might include one table with information about employees and another with information about customers. You don't want to spend a lot of time recreating the structure of the Employees table for the Customers table, and with Access you don't have to. You can copy the structure of an existing table to create a new one. Here's how to copy the Employees table structure to create the Customers table:

Copying a table's structure

1. Close the Employees table, and with Employees selected in the Database window, click the Copy button on the toolbar.

2. Click the Paste button on the toolbar to display the Paste Table As dialog box. Type *Customers*, select the Structure Only option, and then click OK. Access adds the Customers table to the list in the Database window.

3. Select Customers, and click Design to display the new table in Design view.

Now you need to make some field adjustments:

1. Change the *EmployeeID* field name to *CustomerID*, change the word *employee* in this field's Description column to *customer*, and change this field's Caption property to *Cust#*.

Editing field names and captions

2. Select the SocialSecurityNumber field by clicking its row selector, and press the Delete key to delete it. Then delete the FirstName and DateHired fields.

3. Change *LastName* to *Name*, change the field size of this field to *30*, delete the input mask, and change the Caption property to *Name*.

4. Change the *HomePhone* field name to *Phone*.

5. Add a new field called *Log* at the end of the list. After typing Log as the field name, press Enter to move to the Data Type column. Click the arrow, and select Memo from the drop-down list. Press Enter, and type *Interaction record* in the Description column. The table structure now looks like this:

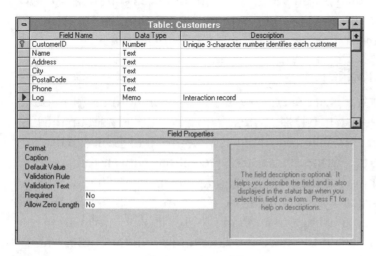

Editing table structure

If you make a mistake while specifying the table's structure, you can easily correct it. To change an entire field name or description, double-click it to highlight the old entry, and type the new one. To change part of a field name or description, click an insertion point where you need to make the correction, and delete and add new characters as necessary. Keyboard lovers can move from one area to another by pressing the Arrow keys but can change existing information only by retyping entire entries; you have to use the mouse to edit parts of an entry. Entries in the Data Type column can be changed by clicking the old entry and selecting a new data type from the drop-down list.

6. Click the Datasheet View button on the toolbar, and when Access prompts you to save the table, click OK.

7. Enter the information shown here, leaving the Log field blank for now. (We've adjusted the widths of some of the fields so that all the data is visible.)

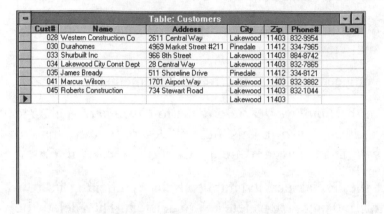

Cust#	Name	Address	City	Zip	Phone#	Log
028	Western Construction Co	2611 Central Way	Lakewood	11403	832-9954	
030	Durahomes	4969 Market Street #211	Pinedale	11412	334-7965	
033	Shurbuilt Inc	966 8th Street	Lakewood	11403	884-8742	
034	Lakewood City Const Dept	28 Central Way	Lakewood	11403	832-7865	
035	James Bready	511 Shoreline Drive	Pinedale	11412	334-8121	
041	Marcus Wilson	1701 Airport Way	Lakewood	11403	832-3882	
045	Roberts Construction	734 Stewart Road	Lakewood	11403	832-1044	
			Lakewood	11403		

Copying the structure of simple tables is relatively easy, but as you begin to create more complex tables, you'll need to consider carefully such characteristics as primary keys and validation rules, as well as the applicability of other Access table features such as referential integrity, which we discuss on page 49. In the meantime, you can see that this technique is a great way of streamlining the table-creation process.

More About Data Types

The Employees table we created in Chapter 1 consisted primarily of text fields with one number field and one date/time field. These data types are the most common, but as you already know, Access offers several others. In this section, we'll see when and how to use the memo and OLE object types.

Memo Fields

Memo fields are useful because they can hold large amounts of data—up to 64,000 bytes. You have already set up the Log field in the Customers table as a memo field. You can use that field to record meetings and conversations with customers about such things as the promised completion date of a job, the date a contract was received, or the name of the person who approved a change to a job in progress. Any information that could be useful down the road could go in this field. Follow these steps to make an entry in the Log field:

1. Increase both the height and width of the Log field to allow space for your entries (see page 18 for more information).

2. In the record for customer number 28, click an insertion point in the Log field, and type the first paragraph shown here:

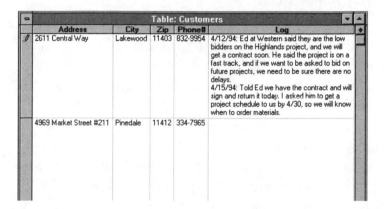

3. To end the first paragraph, press Ctrl+Enter. (Pressing Enter by itself moves you to the Cust# field of the next record.) Then type the second paragraph.

4. Select the Log column by clicking the field name, and then restore the default row height by choosing Row Height from the Format menu and clicking first Standard Height and then OK. Decrease the column width by choosing Column Width from the Format menu, typing *15* in the edit box, and clicking OK. Here's the result:

Cust#	Name	Address	City	Zip	Phone#	Log
028	Western Construction Co	2611 Central Way	Lakewood	11403	832-9954	4/12/94: Ed at
030	Durahomes	4969 Market Street #211	Pinedale	11412	334-7965	
033	Shurbuilt Inc	966 8th Street	Lakewood	11403	884-8742	
034	Lakewood City Const Dept	28 Central Way	Lakewood	11403	832-7865	
035	James Bready	511 Shoreline Drive	Pinedale	11412	334-8121	
041	Marcus Wilson	1701 Airport Way	Lakewood	11403	832-3882	
045	Roberts Construction	734 Stewart Road	Lakewood	11403	832-1044	
			Lakewood	11403		

In the Log field of the first record, you can now see the first part of the entry. If at any time you want to see more of the

If accuracy is important

While entering data in memo fields is not difficult, such tools as spell checkers and thesaurus programs are not available. You might want to type your entries in a word-processing program and then cut and paste them to the memo field in Access.

entry, you can simply enlarge the field both horizontally and vertically.

5. Close the Customers table, clicking Yes to save your changes.

OLE Object Fields

How OLE object fields work

When you want to include an element such as a graphic in a field, you have to assign the field the OLE object data type. You can then embed the graphic from an application that supports OLE (*object linking and embedding*) in the OLE object field, thereby creating a link between the graphic and the source application. When you want to update the graphic, you simply double-click the OLE object field in the table to open the source application, where you can edit the graphic. Closing the source application updates the OLE object field. Follow these steps to create a new table that includes an OLE object field:

1. In the Database window, click the New button, click the New Table button to display a blank table structure window, and then define the table as shown here:

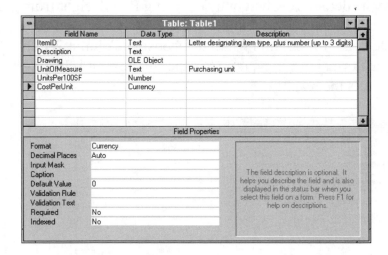

2. Click the row selector for the ItemID field to select the row, and make this field the primary key by clicking the Set Primary Key button on the toolbar.

3. Assign a field size of 4 to the ItemID field, type *Item#* in the Caption edit box, and set the Required property to Yes.

4. Assign a field size of 10 to the UnitOfMeasure field, type *Unit of Measure* in the Caption edit box, and set the Required property to Yes.

5. For the UnitsPer100SF field, type a caption of *Units Per 100 SF*. Then for the CostPerUnit field, type a caption of *Cost Per Unit*. Set the Required properties of both fields to Yes.

6. Click the Datasheet View button, click OK when Access tells you to save the table structure, type *Materials* as the name of the table in the Save As dialog box, and press Enter.

7. Now enter the data shown here. Leave the Drawing field empty for now, and try holding down the Ctrl key and pressing the ' (single quotation mark) key to repeat the value from the field above in the current field, instead of constantly typing identical entries.

Repeating field values

Table: Materials

Item#	Description	Drawing	Unit of Measure	Units Per 100	Cost Per Unit
F01	Flashing: Galvanized flat		IN FT	0	$0.26
F02	Flashing: Galvanized 90		LN FT	0	$0.29
F03	Flashing: Galvanized drip		LN FT	12	$0.40
N01	Nails: Galvanized 7/8"		LB	0.6	$0.76
N02	Nails: Galvanized 1"		LB	0.6	$0.89
P01	Paper: Heavyweight		Roll	1	$13.00
P02	Paper: Standard		Roll	1	$6.50
S01	Shingles: Cedar standard		Bundle	4	$7.00
S02	Shingles: Cedar premium		Bundle	4	$9.00
S03	Shingles: Asphalt		Square	1	$19.50
				0	$0.00

Record: 11 of 11

Now let's see how to use this table's OLE object field to store a graphic. The Drawing field in the Materials table is an OLE object field in which you can store images such as parts, floor plans, art work, instructional drawings, and so on. As a demonstration, we'll create a couple of simple drawings in Paintbrush and embed them in the table. Here are the steps:

1. Click the Drawing field for item N01, and choose Insert Object from the Edit menu. Access displays the dialog box shown on the next page.

Creating a graphic

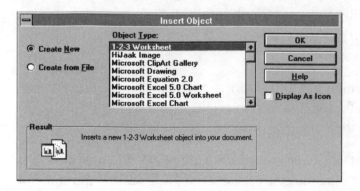

2. Scroll the Object Type list, select Paintbrush Picture, and click OK to display a Paintbrush window.

3. Using the Oval and Line tools, draw a nail similar to this one (drawing isn't our strong suit, as you can see):

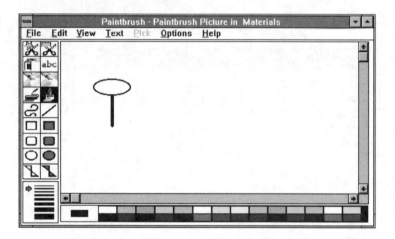

Embedding a graphic

4. Double-click the Control menu icon in the top left corner to close Paintbrush (there is no need to save the drawing). Access displays this dialog box:

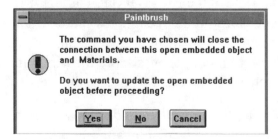

5. Click Yes to update the object in the Drawing field. Though you can't see it, your drawing is now part of the Materials table, as shown here:

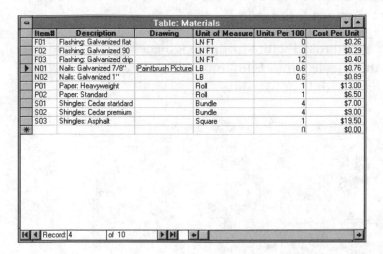

6. Repeat steps 1 through 5 to create the following drawing for item S03 (an asphalt shingle):

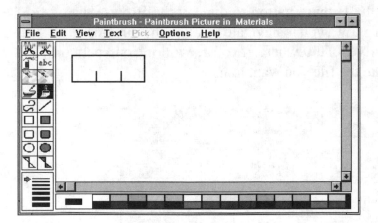

To see a graphic, all you need to do is double-click its field to open it in a Paintbrush window, where you can make any necessary changes. Closing the Paintbrush window after making changes displays the dialog box shown on the facing page. Click Yes to update the field.

Viewing a graphic

For these two examples, you created small drawings to put in the table. You can also paste existing images directly into

OLE object fields. Follow these steps to use one of the images that comes with Windows:

Embedding existing graphics →

1. Click the Drawing field for item F01, and then choose Insert Object from the Edit menu.

2. Select Paintbrush Picture from the Object Type list, and then click the Create From File button. The Insert Object dialog box changes to look like this:

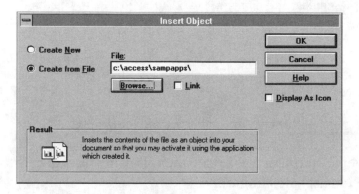

Browsing for a file →

3. Click the Browse button to display the Browse dialog box, which allows you to navigate through the directories on your hard drive (or elsewhere, if you're working on a network) and indicate the file you want to use:

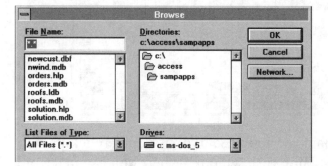

4. In the Directories list, double-click C:\ to list all the directories on your C drive. Scroll the list, and double-click the Windows folder icon to list the files stored in the WINDOWS directory. Scroll the File Name list, and double-click RIVETS.BMP (or any other BMP file).

5. Now click OK in the Insert Object dialog box to embed the graphic in the Materials table.

Graphic restraint

Bitmap graphic files are often quite large, and using graphic fields can quickly eat up disk space as well as impact your computer's performance. Think twice about the usefulness of graphic fields before you load up your system with images that look pretty but serve little practical purpose.

6. Double-click item F01's Drawing field to verify that the graphic is indeed embedded in the field, close the Paintbrush window, and then close the Materials table, saving your changes when prompted.

Establishing Table Relationships

With Access, you can create relationships between tables so that you can combine the data from more than one table in queries, forms, and reports. Usually the relationships involve tables in which the primary key of one table matches a field called the *foreign key* in another table. You can think of the table with the primary key as the *parent* and the table with the foreign key as the *child*. Usually the values in the foreign key field don't have to be unique, but each one must match a value in the parent's primary key field. Access provides a method called *referential integrity* for ensuring that the field values match.

Foreign keys

Referential integrity

To demonstrate referential integrity, we'll create a new table called Estimates. Follow these steps:

1. Click New in the Database window, click the New Table button, and create the following table structure:

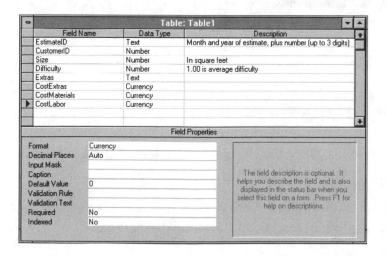

Field Name	Data Type	Description
EstimateID	Text	Month and year of estimate, plus number (up to 3 digits)
CustomerID	Number	
Size	Number	In square feet
Difficulty	Number	1.00 is average difficulty
Extras	Text	
CostExtras	Currency	
CostMaterials	Currency	
CostLabor	Currency	

Field Properties

Format	Currency
Decimal Places	Auto
Input Mask	
Caption	
Default Value	0
Validation Rule	
Validation Text	
Required	No
Indexed	No

The field description is optional. It helps you describe the field and is also displayed in the status bar when you select this field on a form. Press F1 for help on descriptions.

2. Make the EstimateID field the primary key.

3. Assign the fields the properties shown on the next page.

Field name rules

The field names in any one table must be unique and cannot be longer than 64 characters. You can use any combination of characters except periods, exclamation marks, single back quote marks, and square brackets.

Field	Field Size	Decimal Places	Caption	Required
EstimateID	10		Est#	Yes
CustomerID	Byte		Cust#	Yes
Size	Long Integer			Yes
Difficulty	Single			
Extras	25			
CostExtras		2	Extras Cost	
CostMaterials		2	Materials Cost	Yes
CostLabor		2	Labor Cost	Yes

4. Set the Difficulty field's Default Value property to 1.

5. Double-click the Control menu icon to close the window, and save the new table with the name *Estimates* when prompted.

Now let's create a referential integrity relationship between the Customers and Estimates tables:

1. With the Database window active, click the Relationships button on the toolbar to display this dialog box:

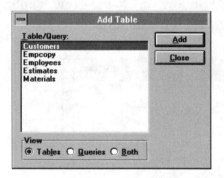

In the Table/Query list, Access has selected the Customers table.

2. Click the Add button. Access adds a Customers box to the blank window behind the Add Table dialog box.

3. Click Estimates, click Add, and then click Close. Access displays the Relationships window. (If your window fills the entire screen, it simply means the window is maximized. You can click the Restore button at the right end of the menu bar—not the title bar—to reduce the size of the window as shown here.)

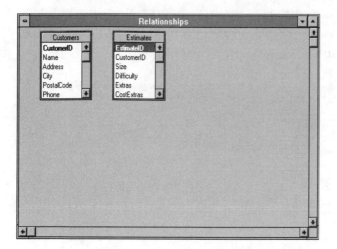

4. In the Customers box, point to the CustomerID field name, hold down the left mouse button, drag the field icon to the CustomerID field name in the Estimates box, and release the mouse button. Access displays this dialog box:

Linking the tables

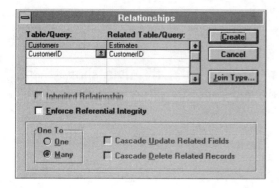

5. Click the Enforce Referential Integrity option to tell Access to require that values in the CustomerID field in the Estimates table match values in the same field in the Customers table.

Enforcing referential integrity

6. Leave the Many option selected in the One To section to tell Access that for each record in the parent table (Customers), there can be many records with a matching field value in the child table (Estimates). The other One To option, One, means that each record in the parent table can have only one record with a matching value in the child table.

One to many

One to one

7. Click the Create button to create the new relationship between the tables. Access draws a line connecting the two fields in the Relationships window, like this:

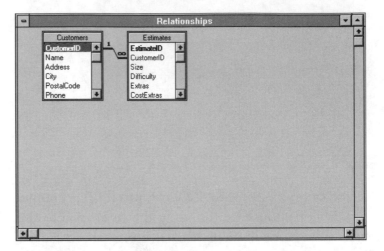

8. Close the Relationships window, saving the changes to the database when prompted.

Here's the acid test:

Testing referential integrity 1. Open the Estimates table, and enter the data shown here, leaving the Material Cost and Labor Cost fields empty for now:

Est#	Cust#	Size	Difficulty	Extras	Extras Cost
E02-94-01	33	1850	1.1	Redo damaged trim	$640.00
E02-94-02	45	18200	0.95	New trim	$800.00
E02-94-03	28	2200	1	None	$0.00
E02-94-04	35	2430	1	None	$0.00
E02-94-05	30	1550	1	None	$0.00
E02-94-06	33	2710	1	None	$0.00
E02-94-07	41	1220	1	Chimney cap	$120.00
E02-94-08	28	2260	1	None	$0.00
E02-94-09	33	1750	1	None	$0.00
E02-94-10	45	18200	0.95	New trim	$800.00
E03-94-01	28	1950	1	None	$0.00
E03-94-02	45	2100	1.05	New gutters	$710.00
E03-94-03	30	1450	0.9	None	$0.00
E03-94-04	30	1450	0.9	None	$0.00
E03-94-06	30	2200	1	None	$0.00
E03-94-07	34	4100	1.1	Trim two trees	$380.00
E04-94-01	33	2480	1	New gutters	$590.00
	0	0	1		$0.00

Record: 18   of 18

The EstimateID field values

You may be wondering why the EstimateID field values are not simple numbers. You can often use fields such as this one to hold information that would otherwise require an additional field. Here the EstimateID field values record the month and year in which the estimate was made, followed by a sequential number that makes each value unique.

2. Try entering an incorrect customer number. You can type any number in the field, but Access won't let you leave the record until a correct customer number is in place.

Now that you have created this referential integrity relationship, you cannot change the CustomerID values in the Customers table. If you need to change one of these values, you must first delete the relationship.

Multiple Table Relationships

As you have seen, establishing a relationship between two tables is simple. Now let's get fancy and create relationships that will enable us to use the data from several tables. We have already created Customers and Estimates tables for the sample roofing company, but the company cannot make money unless some of those estimates become actual jobs. To track these jobs, we'll create a Jobs table that is related to both the Customers and Estimates tables. Follow these steps to create the new table and add the relationships:

1. Close the Estimates table, click New in the Database window, and then click the New Table button.

2. Enter the following table structure:

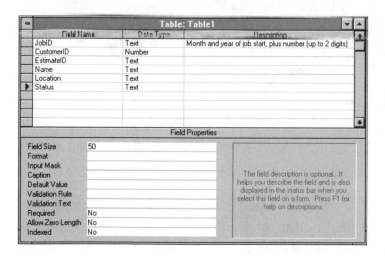

3. Make the JobID field the primary key and a required field.

4. Assign field sizes of 8 to the JobID field, Byte to the CustomerID field, 10 to the EstimateID field, and 25 to the Name, Location, and Status fields.

5. Assign these captions:

Job# to JobID
Cust# to CustomerID
Est# to EstimateID

6. Double-click the Control menu icon to close the Table window, and when prompted, save the table with the name *Jobs*.

Now create the relationships to the Customers and Estimates tables by following these steps:

1. With the Database window active, click the Relationships button on the toolbar.

2. When the Relationships window appears, click the Add Table button on the toolbar, select Jobs, click the Add button, and then click Close. Access adds a box for the Jobs table to the Relationships window, like this:

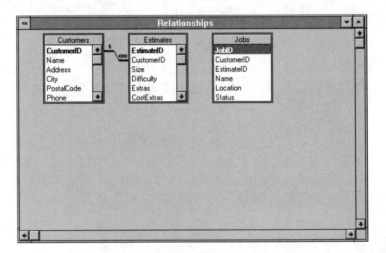

Viewing relationships

Sometimes the relationships between tables are hard to see in the Relationships window because of the way the table boxes are positioned. You can move the table boxes by dragging their title bars, just as you would drag a dialog box or window.

3. Click the CustomerID field in the Customers box, hold down the left mouse button, drag across to the CustomerID field in the Jobs box, and release the mouse button. Then in the Relationships dialog box, select the Enforce Referential Integrity option, and click Create to create the new relationship as one to many.

4. Repeat step 3, this time dragging from the EstimateID field in the Estimates box to the EstimateID field in the Jobs box. After you select Enforce Referential Integretity and click the

Create button, the Relationships window looks like the one shown here:

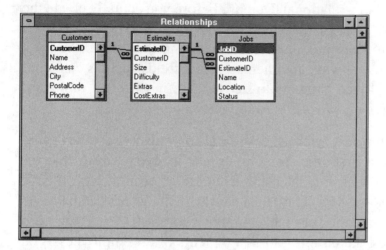

5. Double-click the Control menu icon to close the Relationships window, clicking Yes when Access asks whether you want to save your changes.

You will now be able to take advantage of these relationships as you work through the rest of the book. In the meantime, let's complete the Jobs table:

1. In the Database window, select Jobs, and click the Open button.

2. Adjust the column widths, and enter this information in the table, being sure to include *downs* with a lowercase *d* as shown here:

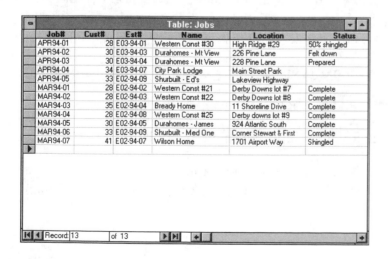

The JobID field values

Like the EstimateID field values, the JobID field values are not simple numbers. We have used this field to indicate the job's starting date. Notice that the sequential number that makes each field value unique is preceded by a zero. That way, if the company starts more than nine jobs in a given month, the jobs are listed in numeric order. Without the zero, the order would be 1, 10, 11, ... 2, 20, 21, ...3, 30, 31, and so on.

3. When you have entered all the data, close the Jobs table.

Data modeling →

Often you will make decisions about the data relationships needed in a relational database before you actually create the tables. Database design involves listing the types of data you want to keep in a database, organizing the data in the most economical way, and then selecting fields such as customer or employee numbers to tie the data in different tables together. This process is called *data modeling*.

Design modifications →

Even the best database designers don't always get the design right the first time. Sometimes you'll have to make changes after you have created the database or even after you have entered the data. This is the case with the Roofs database. As you create the Jobs table, suppose you realize that you need to track the current job assignments of all employees. You can't add an EmployeeID field to the Jobs table because several employees might be assigned to the same job. Instead, you will have to modify the Employees table to include a JobID field. The process involves changing the design of the Employees table, adding another relationship, and entering job numbers in the Employees table. Follow these steps:

1. In the Database window, click Employees and then click the Design button to open the table in Design view.

2. Select the First Name field by clicking its row selector, and press the Insert key to add a new blank row above First Name.

3. Type *JobID* as the new field name, specify Text as the data type, type *Foreign key* as the description, and assign a field size of 8 and a caption of *Job#*.

4. Close the Employees table, saving the changes when prompted.

Now let's add another relationship to the database:

1. Click the Relationships button on the toolbar.

2. When the Relationships window appears, click the Add Table button, select Employees, and click the Add button and then the Close button.

Exporting data

To export the data in an Access table for use in another program, choose Export from the File menu. Access then walks you through the steps for creating a file in the format you select. If you are unsure of the format to use, select Text [Delimited], a common format that most applications can work with.

3. Now drag the JobID field in the Jobs box to the JobID field in the Employees box, click Enforce Referential Integrity, and then click Create to add this one to many relationship to the database.

4. Close the Relationships window, clicking Yes to save your changes.

All you have left to do is add the job numbers to the Employees table:

1. Open the Employees table, and enter the job numbers shown here, leaving the field for Carol Talbot blank, because she works in the office:

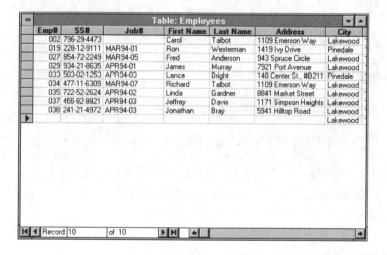

Emp#	SS#	Job#	First Name	Last Name	Address	City
002	796-29-4473		Carol	Talbot	1109 Emerson Way	Lakewood
019	228-12-9111	MAR94-01	Ron	Westerman	1419 Ivy Drive	Pinedale
027	854-72-2249	MAR94-05	Fred	Anderson	943 Spruce Circle	Lakewood
029	934-21-8635	APR94-01	James	Murray	7921 Port Avenue	Lakewood
033	503-02-1253	APR94-03	Lance	Bright	140 Center St., #B211	Pinedale
034	477-11-6309	MAR94-07	Richard	Talbot	1109 Emerson Way	Lakewood
035	722-52-2624	APR94-02	Linda	Gardner	8841 Market Street	Lakewood
037	455-82-9921	APR94-03	Jeffrey	Davis	1171 Simpson Heights	Lakewood
038	241-21-4972	APR94-03	Jonathan	Bray	5941 Hilltop Road	Lakewood
						Lakewood

Record: 10   of 10

2. Close the table.

Validation Rules

In Chapter 1, we discussed all of the field properties that are available when designing tables except the Validation Rule and Validation Text properties. When you set a validation rule for a field, Access allows only field values that meet the rule to be entered in the field. The kind of rule you can set up varies with the field's data type. You can specify that a text field should contain one of a set of values—for example, the City field should contain only Pinedale or Lakewood. You can

Importing data

Access can import data in various formats. Choose Import from the File menu, and then complete a series of dialog boxes to locate the data's file and if necessary, specify the structure of the table in which the data will be stored. Instead of using the Import command, you can click the Attach Table button to establish a link with a table in another Access database or in another database program. The table is accessible from the Database window by clicking its name, which has an arrow to its left and is also accessible from within its source database or database program.

specify that a date field should contain only the current date or a date that falls within a certain range. With number fields, you can specify that Access should accept only a specific value, or you can use the greater than (>) and less than (<) signs to specify that field values must fall within a range. You can also specify that the values in a field must match the values in the same field in another table. Let's look at some examples.

Suppose the Estimates table includes a Difficulty field that will be used later to adjust the labor cost in the estimates up or down depending on the difficulty of the job. The values in this field should fall between 0.75 and 1.25. A typographical error in this field might produce an estimate that is much higher or much lower than it should be. Using the Validation Rule property, you can avoid this kind of mistake by limiting the allowable field values to a range. Follow these steps to create the necessary rule:

1. Open the Estimates table in Design view.

2. Click anywhere in the Difficulty field's row to select it.

3. Click the Validation Rule edit box in the Field Properties section, and then click the Build button to the right of the edit box. Access displays the Expression Builder dialog box:

Sample validation rule

You can create a validation rule based on another field in the same table. For example, suppose that company policy requires that someone place a follow-up call to the customer five days after each order is shipped. You can create a Follow Up field in which to note when the call must be placed and make the field's Validation Rule property =[ShipDate]+5. Then Access will only let you leave the field blank or type in an entry that is five days after the date entered in the ShipDate field.

4. Click the > button, type .75, click the And button, click the < button, and type 1.25. Then if necessary, delete expr and its enclosing chevrons, which Access may have inserted before the < symbol, and click OK.

5. Click the Validation Text edit box, and type *Value must be between 0.75 and 1.25*. This message will be displayed whenever an unacceptable value is entered.

Explaining rules to users

6. Switch to Datasheet view, save the changes to the table's structure, and click Yes when Access asks whether you want it to test existing data in the Difficulty field against the new rule you just specified.

Now we'll test the new validation rule:

1. Change the Difficulty field value in the first record to 11, and then try moving to the next record. Access displays this message box:

Testing validation rules

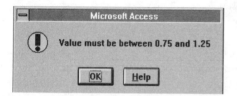

2. Click OK in the message box, and change the Difficulty value to 1.1. Then close the Table window.

As you can see, validation rules are powerful tools that can help you ensure the accuracy of your data. The need for a validation rule may not be apparent when you first create a table; you may identify the need only after problems begin to show up. So it's good to know that you can always go back and add these safeguards later.

Protecting Your Data

If you are running Access on your own computer at work or at home, you probably don't have to worry about the kinds of conflicts that can arise when more than one person has access to the same database. However, if you share a computer, you might have concerns about protecting your data, and if you work on a network, protecting your data becomes a necessity. You can lock a record or an entire database to temporarily control access, and you can create passwords to control access more permanently.

Backing up

Regularly backing up your files is an important aspect of database security. In addition to copying your database files to floppy disks or tape for storage away from your computer, you might want to create a BACKUP directory in which you can store a copy of your working directory to protect against inadvertent changes to the working files.

Unlike many applications that wait for you to tell them when to save information, Access saves the values in a new or edited record as soon as you move to the next record. As a result, on a network two or more people can work on a table at the same time. To prevent someone else from working on the same record as you, you can lock the record, like this:

Locking records

1. Choose Options from the View menu.

2. In the Options dialog box, select the Multiuser/ODBC category to display this list:

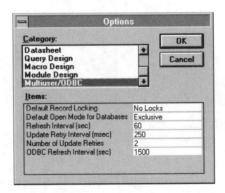

Locking options

3. Click the Default Record Locking edit box, and then click the arrow to see a list of choices. No Locks is the default. The Edited Record option locks the record that is being edited in a datasheet, form, or query. The All Records option locks the record in the open table and all the related tables. (This option can restrict the ability of other people to see the data, so think twice before locking all the records.)

4. We won't apply any locks at this time, so click Cancel to close the Options dialog box.

Locking a database

To prevent someone from working on the same database at the same time, you open the database for exclusive use by clicking the Open Database button on the toolbar, selecting the database from the File Name list, clicking the Exclusive option, and then clicking OK.

Access handles security beyond the simple record-locking and exclusive-use level by assigning users to groups, and then defining what the different groups can do in the tables, forms, reports, and so on that make up a specific database. If you are responsible for database security, see the *Building Applications* manual that comes with Microsoft Access, which explains in detail the multi-step process of protecting databases from unauthorized use.

◄—————— **Database security**

Deleting Tables

In the process of learning how to copy tables, you created a table—Empcopy—that you no longer need. Let's finish this chapter by deleting the table to reduce the size of your database file. Because tables don't exist as independent files, you can delete tables only from within Access and not by using File Manager or the DOS Del command. Follow these steps to ax the table:

1. With the Database window open on your screen, select Empcopy. (You cannot delete a table if it is open.)

2. Choose Delete from the Edit menu. Access displays this warning:

3. Click OK, and Access deletes the table.

   Now that you have a good grasp of database tables, we'll move on to look at some other components of Access databases, starting with queries.

Deletion restrictions

Tables that are the parent in a relationship cannot be deleted. Fields that are used to create a relationship between tables cannot be deleted, and their data types cannot be changed. If you need to delete a table or change or delete a field, you must first delete the relationship in the Relationships window.

3
Using Queries
to Extract Information

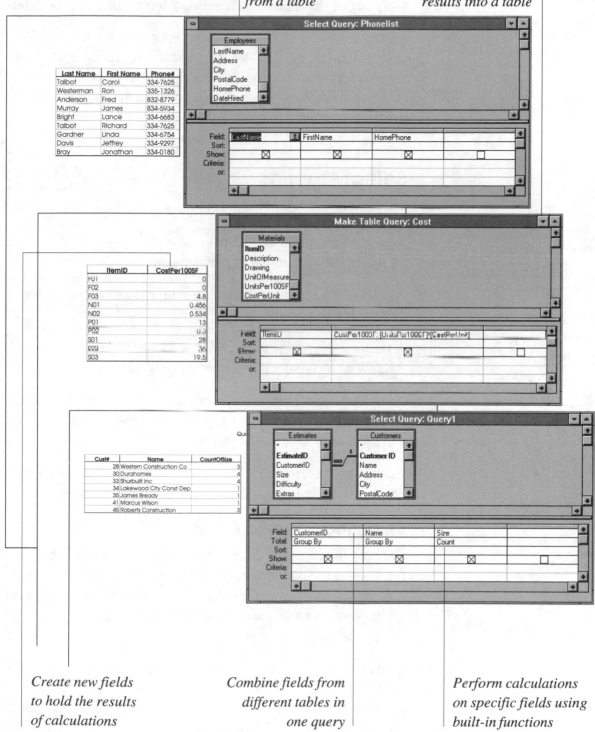

Use a select query to extract fields from a table

Use a make table query to convert query results into a table

Create new fields to hold the results of calculations

Combine fields from different tables in one query

Perform calculations on specific fields using built-in functions

I n Access, you use queries to ask questions about your database tables, to extract complete or partial records from the tables, and even to edit records. Queries that find and extract information from a database are called *select queries*, and queries that perform an action such as updating or deleting records are called *action queries*.

In this chapter, we'll look first at some select queries and then at some action queries, using both simple single-table and more complex multi-table examples. Four other types of queries— union, parameter, crosstab, and pass-through —are explained briefly in tips throughout the chapter.

Select queries

Action queries

Other types of queries

Select Queries

Here are some examples of common select queries:

Query examples

- A supervisor might want a list of the emergency contacts for all the employees in his or her department.

- A sales manager might want to see the records for sales over a certain dollar amount.

- A training instructor might want to identify classes for which too few or too many people have enrolled.

- A purchasing officer might want a list of vendors who carry all the supplies needed for a particular job so that one order can be placed instead of several.

Access answers these queries by selecting a subset of records and fields and placing them in a temporary datasheet.

Query datasheets

Selecting Specific Fields

Suppose the roofing company's job supervisor has asked you for a list of the phone numbers of company employees. He is not interested in any other information about the employees; all he wants is names and phone numbers. You can create the list by following these steps:

1. Open the Roofs database, and in the Database window, click the Query button and then click New. In the New Query dialog box, click New Query. Access opens a Select Query window and displays the Add Table dialog box.

2. Select Employees, click Add to add the table to the Select
Query window, and then click Close to close the dialog box.
The Select Query window now looks like this:

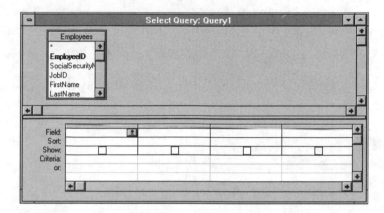

The Employees box lists the fields in the Employees table.
(The * at the top of the list represents the entire table.) Below
is a table grid called the *query by example (QBE) grid*, in
which you can visually structure the query.

Query by example grid

3. In the Employees box, double-click the LastName field name
to tell Access to include LastName field values in the answer
to your query. Access transfers the LastName field to the first
column of the QBE grid's Field row, displaying its caption
and putting an X in the box in the Show row to indicate that
LastName field values should appear in the query datasheet.

4. In the Employees box, double-click FirstName to transfer it
to the second column of the grid's Field row. Then scroll the
Employees box, and double-click the HomePhone field
name. (If you double-click the wrong field name, press the
Delete key to delete the highlighted entry, and then try again.)

5. With the Show boxes of these three fields selected, click the
Run button on the toolbar. The result is this datasheet:

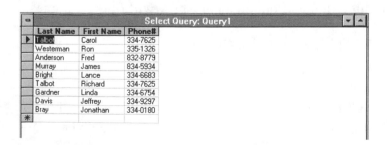

6. Print the query datasheet by clicking the Print button on the toolbar and clicking OK in the Print dialog box. You can then give the phone-number list to the job supervisor.

The datasheet and the query that created it are temporary. To be able to run this query periodically without having to recreate it every time, you must save the query. Here's how:

Saving queries

1. Choose Save Query As from the File menu to display the Save As dialog box:

2. In the Query Name edit box, type *Phonelist* as the name of the query, and press Enter.

3. Close the Select Query window.

The Database window now lists Phonelist as an existing query. Any time you want to access the datasheet of the names and phone numbers of the roofing company's employees, you can select this query and click Open. Access runs the query and opens a datasheet. If you have made changes to the Employee table, these changes will be reflected in the datasheet.

If you need to change the design of the query to produce different results, you can do it easily by following these steps:

Modifying queries

1. With Phonelist selected in the Database window, click the Design button to display the query in Design view.

2. Click the box in the Show row of the LastName column to tell Access not to display last names in the query datasheet.

3. Click the Run button on the toolbar. Access runs the query and produces a new Phonelist datasheet without last names.

Selecting Specific Records

You now know how to ask questions that require Access to select fields from a table. What if you want Access to select fields only from specific records? For example, suppose that the shingles for job number APR94-03 are going to be delivered late and you need the employees assigned to that job to report to the office in the morning instead of the job site. Follow these steps to modify the Phonelist query so that Access will include in the query datasheet only the names and phone numbers of the employees assigned to job APR94-03:

1. Click the Design View button to switch the Phonelist query to Design view, and then double-click JobID in the Employees box to add it to the QBE grid.

Adding fields to queries

2. In the Show row, click the box for the LastName field to select it, and then click the box for the JobID field to deselect it.

3. In the Criteria row of the JobID column, type *APR94-03*. The query now looks like this:

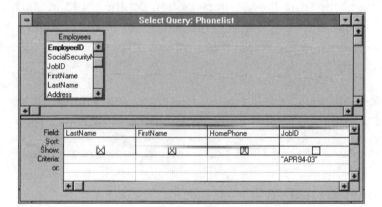

You are telling Access to give you the names and phone numbers from the records that have the value APR94-03 in the JobID field. (The JobID field value will not appear in the query datasheet because that field's Show box is not selected.)

4. Run the query to create this new Phonelist datasheet:

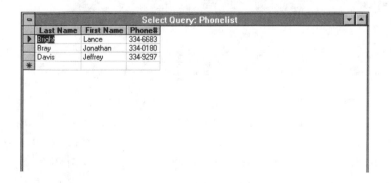

Keeping track of fields

If you are working with several tables, it can be difficult to keep track of which fields belong to which tables. To avoid confusion, add a Table row to the QBE grid by clicking the Table Names button on the toolbar. Access adds a row below the Field row, displaying the table names for all the fields.

Using the Phonelist datasheet, you can now call the three employees assigned to job number APR94-03 and tell them to report to the office in the morning.

5. Close the Select Query window without saving the changes to the PhoneList query.

Using Wildcards

Let's try another query, this time using the Jobs table. Suppose you want Access to tell you the status of all the roofing jobs in Derby Downs, but you think the Derby Downs entries in the Location field are inconsistent. Here's how to get the information you need:

1. In the Database window, click the Table button, select the Jobs table, click the New Query button on the toolbar, and then click New Query. This technique opens a Select Query window based on the Jobs table without displaying the Add Table dialog box.

2. Double-click the JobID, Name, Location, and Status field names to add those fields to the QBE grid.

Querying with wildcards

3. In the Criteria row of the Location field, type *Derby**, and then click anywhere in the QBE grid or press Enter. Access converts your criterion as shown here:

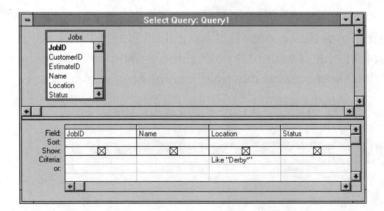

As you can see, Access has converted the criterion to *Like "Derby*"*, indicating that it will search for field values that begin with Derby. The * is a wildcard that stands for any number and any type of character. *Like* is an operator that tells Access not to look for an exact match.

The Like operator

4. Run the query. Access creates a datasheet containing these records for Derby Downs:

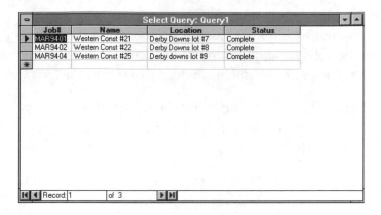

You can place the * wildcard before, after, and between characters, and you can use it more than once in a single field. For example, you could have typed *D*D** in the Location field to find jobs in Derby Downs. As you can imagine, the * wildcard is useful when you need to find records that are similar but not the same.

The * wildcard

In addition to *, you can use the ? wildcard as a placeholder for one character. For example, you could extract all the records for shingles from the Materials table by using the criterion *"Like S0?"* in the ItemID field of a query.

The ? wildcard

Both the * and the ? wildcards can be used to locate records when you are unsure of the spelling of a field value. For example, one of the job names in the Jobs table is *Bready*, which might be an unusual spelling or might be a typo. If the Jobs table contained many records with Name field values starting with *Br*, it could be time-consuming to find the Bready record, even using *br** in a query. You can make short work of this task by using the criterion *Br*dy** to locate all the records that begin with *Br* and contain *dy* somewhere else in the field value. As you can see, the more information you can supply, the more specific the query datasheet will be.

Editing Query Datasheets

If you entered the information for the Jobs table exactly as it is shown on page 55, the datasheet now on your screen indicates a typo in the third Derby Downs record (*downs* should be *Downs*). Correcting the record in the datasheet will automatically correct it in the table. Try this:

1. Choose Database from the Window menu to display the Database window, click Table, select Jobs, and then click Open. In the Jobs table, job number MAR94-04 has a Location field value of *Derby downs* instead of *Derby Downs*.

2. Choose Select Query from the Window menu, click an insertion point to the right of the *d* in *downs*, press Backspace, type *D*, and click a different record.

3. Choose Table from the Window menu. Job number MAR94-04 now has a Location field value of *Derby Downs*.

Using Logical Operators

You can narrow down the data Access pulls from a database table by specifying criteria in more than one field of a Select Query grid. Sometimes you might want to extract records that meet all the criteria in all the fields (this And that), and sometimes you might want to extract records that meet any criterion in any field (this Or that). Let's look at a few examples.

The And Operator

Suppose you need to know which of the Durahomes jobs is complete so that you can bill the customer; that is, you want to see records that are both for Durahomes and complete. In Access, the And operator is implied whenever you use more than one criterion in a single row of the Select Query window. Follow these steps to extract the required record:

1. Display the Select Query window containing the Jobs datasheet, and click the Design View button to switch to Design view.

2. Click the criterion in the Location field, press F2 to select the criterion, and press Delete.

3. Double-click the CustomerID field to add it to the QBE grid, scroll the window, type *30* as a criterion in the CustomerID field's Criteria row, and type *Complete* as a criterion in the Status field. The Select Query window now looks like this:

Customizing the Query window

To quickly remove a table from the Query window, click the title bar of the table's box and press the Delete key. If you have several tables in the window and need to rearrange them to see the relationships better, simply drag their title bars to move them around. If you need more room for the table boxes or for the table grid, you can click and drag the line that separates the two areas of the Query window.

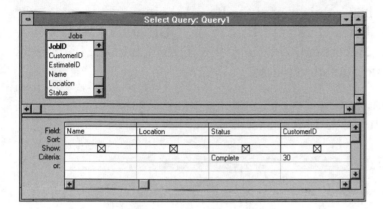

4. Run the query. Access displays the record for the complete Durahomes job:

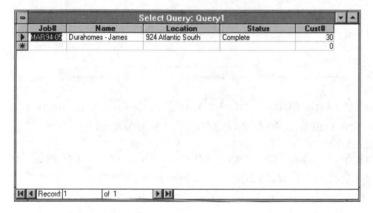

The Or Operator

Now suppose you want to negotiate new prices for roofing shingles and felt paper with suppliers, and you want Access to pull the current prices for those items from the Materials table. Shingles have item numbers that begin with *S* and types of felt paper have item numbers that begin with *P*, so you want to see records that have ItemID field values starting with *S* or *P*. Follow these steps:

1. Close any open Select Query windows without saving them, and close the Jobs table. In the Database window, select Materials in the table list, click the New Query button on the toolbar, and then click New Query.

2. Double-click the ItemID, Description, and CostPerUnit field names to include those fields in the query datasheet.

Or rows

In the QBE grid, only one row is designated as an Or row. However, the Or operator is implied for all the rows below the Or row. If you need to use more Or criteria, enter them in successive rows.

3. Click the Criteria row of the ItemID column, and type *S* Or P**, and then click anywhere in the QBE grid or press Enter. Again, Access converts your criteria to include the Like operator and quotation marks.

4. Run the query. Access creates a datasheet that contains only these items and their prices:

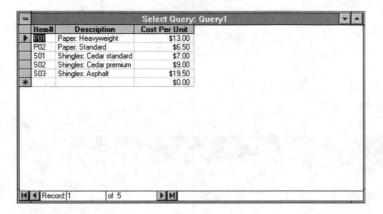

You can now print the prices so that you will have them on hand when you talk to the company's suppliers.

What if you want to select records that meet criteria in different fields? For example, suppose you want Access to select from the Jobs table the records with a value of *Durahomes - Mt. View* in the Name field or a value of *High Ridge Road* in the Location field because these jobs are in the same neighborhood. Here are the steps:

Removing tables from the Query window

1. Click the Design View button to switch to Design view, click the Materials box, and then choose Remove Table from the Query menu.

2. Click the Add Table button on the toolbar to display the Add Table dialog box, double-click Jobs to add that table's fields to the Select Query window, and close the dialog box.

3. Double-click the Name and Location field names to move those fields to the QBE grid.

4. Type *"Dura* - Mt View"* in the Criteria row of the Name field. (The criterion includes spaces, so you must enclose it in quotation marks.)

5. Because the And operator is implied when you enter criteria in two or more fields in the same row, you must enter the second criterion in the Or row of the Location field. Type *"High Ridge*"* to find entries for both High Ridge Road and High Ridge Rd. The query window looks like this:

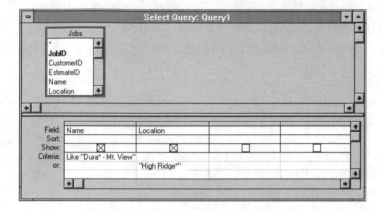

6. Run the query. The datasheet includes the records that meet either of your selection criteria.

The Not and Null Operators

You use the Not operator to identify the records that don't meet a specified criterion and the Null operator to identify the records that have no value in a specific field. For example, you can tell Access to identify all the jobs in the Jobs table that are not complete, like this:

1. Click the Design View button to switch to Design view, and double-click the Status field to add it to the QBE grid.

2. Delete the criteria for the Name and Location fields.

3. In the Criteria row of the Status field, type *Not "Complete"* to find the records with Status field values that are something other than *Complete*.

Using Not

4. In the Or row of the Status field, type *Null* to find the records that have no value at all in the Status field.

Using Null

5. Run the query. The new datasheet contains the records for the jobs that are not complete.

Using Mathematical Operators

Access allows you to use mathematical operators in criteria, including = (equal to), < (less than), > (greater than), <= (less than or equal to), and >= (greater than or equal to). These operators are often used for such tasks as identifying employees whose salaries fall within a certain range or locating high-volume customers. Here, let's try using a mathematical operator with a date field to find all the employees who were hired before 1990:

Extracting records with mathematical operators

1. Close any open Select Query windows without saving their queries, and then open a new query for the Employees table.

2. Double-click the FirstName, LastName, and DateHired fields to transfer them to the QBE grid.

3. In the Criteria row of the DateHired column, type *<1/1/90*.

4. Run the query. Access displays a datasheet for the three employees who were hired before 1990.

You can narrow the results down even further by using a range. Display the records for employees who were hired in 1991 by following these steps:

1. Click the Design View button on the toolbar to switch to Design view, and change the entry in the DateHired field to *>12/31/90 And <1/1/92*.

2. Run the query. Now the records for employees hired in 1991 are displayed in the datasheet.

Sorting with Queries

Query Wizards

The Query Wizards help you create queries that perform the following tasks: display data in crosstab format; find duplicate records; find records in one table that do not have matches in another table; and put records from an existing table in a new table.

A basic feature of databases is the ability to sort data so that you can look at it in different ways. For example, the Employees table is currently sorted in ascending order based on the primary key, the EmployeeID field. In Chapter 2, we briefly mentioned that you can sort databases using the Sort Ascending and Sort Descending buttons (see page 40). Using a query, you can sort the table based on the LastName field, as follows:

1. Click the Design View button to switch to Design view, and then choose Clear Grid from the Edit menu to delete the fields from the QBE grid.

Clearing the QBE grid

2. Double-click the title bar of the Employees box to select all the field names in the list. Then point to the selected fields, and hold down the mouse button. When the pointer changes to a stack of boxes, drag it to the QBE grid, and release the mouse button. Access enters the fields in the columns of the grid in the order in which they appear in the list.

Entering all the fields in the grid

3. Click the Sort row of the LastName field, and then click the arrow to the right to display this list of sort order options:

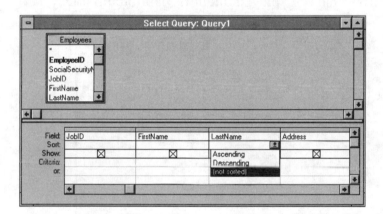

4. Click Ascending, and then run the query. Access sorts the records of the Employees table in ascending order based on the LastName field and displays this datasheet:

Sorting in ascending order

Emp#	SS#	Job#	First Name	Last Name	Address	City
027	854-72-2249	MAR94-05	Fred	Anderson	943 Spruce Circle	Lakewood
038	241-21-4972	APR94-03	Jonathan	Bray	5941 Hilltop Road	Lakewood
033	583-02-1253	APR94-03	Lance	Bright	148 Center St., #B211	Pinedale
037	455-82-9921	APR94-03	Jeffrey	Davis	1171 Simpson Heights	Lakewood
035	722-52-2624	APR94-02	Linda	Gardner	8841 Market Street	Lakewood
029	934-21-8635	APR94-01	James	Murray	7921 Port Avenue	Lakewood
002	796-29-4473		Carol	Talbot	1109 Emerson Way	Lakewood
034	477-11-6309	MAR94-07	Richard	Talbot	1109 Emerson Way	Lakewood
019	228-12-9111	MAR94-01	Ron	Westerman	1419 Ivy Drive	Pinedale
						Lakewood

Record: 1   of 9

Now let's sort the records based on the DateHired field so that you can see the date each employee was hired, starting with the most recent (a descending-order sort):

1. Click the Design View button, and press the Delete key to remove the Sort option from the LastName field.

Sorting in descending order → 2. Scroll the QBE grid until the DateHired field is visible, click its Sort row, click the arrow, and select the Descending option.

3. Run the query. Access sorts the records on the DateHired field with the most recent employee first. (We've adjusted the screen so that you can see all the data. In the datasheet, the DateHired field is displayed under its caption, First Day.)

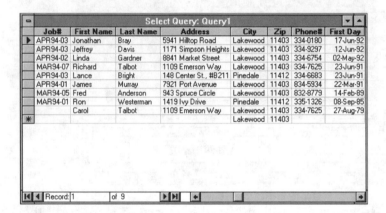

Sometimes you might need to sort using more than one field at a time. For example, if the Employees table was very large, you might have several employees with the same last name, and you might need to use both the first and last names to sort them alphabetically. To demonstrate, we'll sort the datasheet using both the FirstName and LastName fields:

Sorting on multiple fields → 1. Click the Design View button, and press the Delete key to remove the Sort option from the DateHired field.

2. In the Sort row, select the Ascending option for both the First-Name and LastName fields, and run the query.

Oops! That doesn't work. Access sorts first on the FirstName field and then on the LastName field because that's the order in which the fields appear in the QBE grid. To sort first on the LastName field, you need to transpose the two fields:

3. Switch to Design view, point to the LastName field selector—
the gray bar above the column—and when the pointer
changes to a black down arrow, click to select the field. Then
drag the field selector to the left of the FirstName field.

Transposing fields

4. Run the query again. The datasheet is now sorted in descending order by last name with any records having the same
Last-Name value also sorted by first name, as you can see for
the two Talbot records.

Performing Calculations with Selected Records

Sometimes you will want to view calculated summaries of
the information in selected records, not the records themselves. In this section, we'll look at two ways of performing
calculations: using totals queries and using formulas.

Using Totals Queries

Access provides a set of mathematical functions that you can
use to perform standard calculations on number fields without having to detail every step. These functions include the
following:

Mathematical functions

Function	Action
Group By	Group similar field values.
Sum	Totals the values.
Avg	Calculates the average of the values.
Min	Returns the minimum value.
Max	Returns the maximum value.
Count	Counts the values in a field except null values.
Stdev	Returns the standard deviation of the values—a statistical function.
Var	Returns the variance of the field values. This is a statistical function and there must be three or more values to calculate the variance.
First	Returns the value in the first record of a table or query.
Last	Returns the last value.
Expression	Allows an expression (such as <15000) to be used as a criterion for a calculation.
Where	Allows criteria to be established for queries performing calculations.

Some functions work with specific data types. For example, you can use Sum with number and currency fields but not with OLE object or memo fields.

To tell Access to carry out one of these functions on the data in a table, you open a Query window, click the Totals button on the toolbar to add a new Total row to the QBE grid, and then indicate the function you want to use in the appropriate column. Access puts the result in a new field in the query datasheet. Let's use the Estimates table to see the effects of three functions: Count, Avg, and Sum.

1. Close any open Select Query windows without saving the queries, and open a new query for the Estimates table.

Adding a Total row

2. Double-click the Size field to add it to the QBE grid, and then click the Totals button on the toolbar. Access inserts a Total row in the QBE grid and enters *Group By* in the Size column of this row, meaning that by default it will simply group the records in the Estimates table by size.

3. Click the Total row in the Size column, and then click the arrow to drop down a list of Total options:

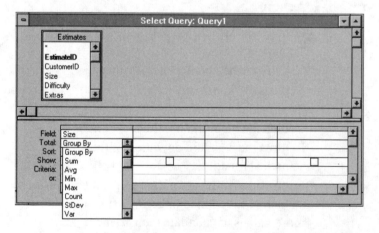

Averaging field values

4. Select Avg from the list, and run the query. The datasheet displays one field with the average size of all the estimates in the table:

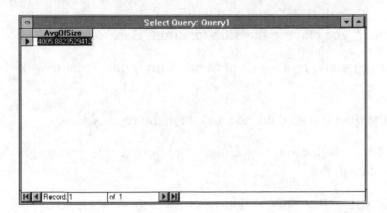

5. Next display the average size per customer by returning to
Design view, double-clicking the CustomerID field in the
Estimates box to add it to the QBE grid, and then running the
query again with the CustomerID field's Total option set to
Group By. Here's the result:

Grouping by customer

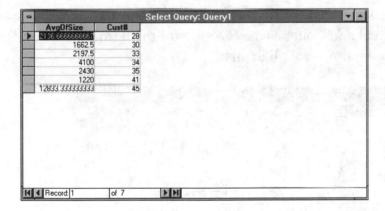

Now suppose you want to know how many estimates you
have prepared for each customer. Follow these steps:

1. Return to Design view, and in the Total row of the Size field,
replace Avg with Count.

Counting field values

2. Run the query. The datasheet now displays the number of
estimates per customer.

Parameter queries

When you run a query, you are often looking for a specific answer, not a whole set of data. For example you might want to see how many jobs the company has done for a specific customer, without displaying that information for all your customers. In addition, you don't want to have to change the criteria when you run this query on a different customer. Fortunately, parameter queries let you run the query and change the parameter on the fly. To set up a parameter query, open a new Query window with the appropriate tables, add the fields to the QBE grid, and set up the Total row to produce the calculation you want (for example, the count of all jobs in the JobID field). Then in the Criteria row, type an instruction to the user (for example, *[Enter a Customer Number]* in the CustomerID field). Close the Query window, saving the query (for example, as *Job Count*). Next, select the query in the Database window, and click the Open button. When prompted in the Enter Parameter Value dialog box, identify the information you want to see (for example, type customer number *33*), and click OK. Parameter queries are fast and powerful. You can even set up multiple parameters by choosing the Parameter command from the Query menu while you are designing your query.

To calculate the total square footage of the estimates for each customer, you can use the Sum function. Here's how:

1. In Design view, replace Count with Sum in the Total row of the Size field.

2. Run the query. The datasheet displays the results.

Here's how to see the Avg, Count, and Sum results in a single query datasheet:

1. Switch to Design view, and move the CustomerID field to the left of the Size field by clicking the CustomerID field selector and then dragging it to the left.

2. In the Estimates box, double-click the Size field to add another Size column to the QBE grid. Then double-click again to add a third Size column.

3. In the Total row, select Avg as the function for the second Size field and Count as the function for the third. The Select Query window looks like this:

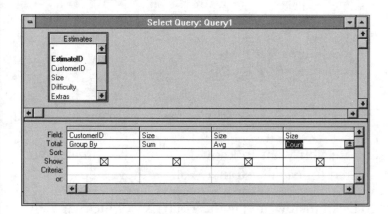

4. Run the query. Access displays all three summary fields in one datasheet where you can easily compare them.

Using Formulas

Often your whole purpose in running a query is to have the values in one field interact with the values in another field in some way. For example, suppose you want to use the values in the UnitsPer100SF and CostPerUnit fields in the Materials table to calculate the cost per 100 square feet of each material. Let's walk through this calculation so that you can see how to use formulas in your own queries:

1. Close any open Select Query windows without saving them, and then open a new query for the Materials table.

2. Double-click the ItemID, UnitsPer100SF, and CostPerUnit fields to add them to the QBE grid.

3. Deselect the Show boxes of the UnitsPer100SF and CostPer-Unit fields so that those fields don't appear in the datasheet.

4. In the Field row, click an insertion point in the fourth column, which is currently blank, and type *[UnitsPer100SF]*[Cost-PerUnit]*, enclosing the field names in square brackets.

Putting the results in a new field

5. Click the Show box for the formula to tell Access to include the results of the formula in the query datasheet.

6. Notice that Access has entered *Expr1* in front of the formula as the name of the new field in which the formula's results will appear. Replace this name with something more meaningful by highlighting Expr1 and typing *CostPer100SF*.

7. Run the query. Access creates a datasheet containing the ItemID field, which has the caption Item#, and the new CostPer100SF field.

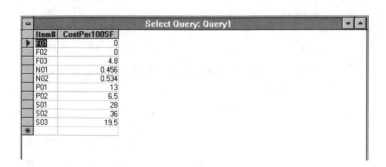

8. Save this query for use later in the chapter, by choosing Save Query As from the File menu, typing *Cost*, and clicking OK.

Using Multiple Tables in Select Queries

As you learned in Chapter 2, when building tables you often include the primary key from one table as a foreign key in other tables so that relationships can be established between the tables. Now we will begin to use related tables in queries so that you can see some of the advantages of a powerful relational database like Access.

Earlier, you queried the Estimates table for information based on the CustomerID field. If the roofing company has many customers, you might want to include the customers' names in the query results, instead of just their numbers. However, the customers' names are not part of the Estimates table; they are stored only in the Customers table. To get the information you want, you must use both tables in a query, like this:

Using two tables

1. Close any open Query windows without saving their queries, and in the Database window, click the Query button, click New, and then click New Query.

2. In the Add Table dialog box, double-click first Estimates and then Customers, and then click the Close button. The Select Query window now contains boxes for both tables. Because we created a relationship between these tables in Chapter 2 (see page 50), Access indicates the relationship in the Select Query window by drawing a line between the CustomerID fields in the two boxes.

3. In the Estimates box, double-click the CustomerID field to add it to the QBE grid; in the Customers box, double-click the Name field; and then in the Estimates box, double-click the Size field.

Quick table addition

You can quickly add a table to the Query window by dragging the table's name from the Database window to the Query window. Access displays a box with all of the table's field names, just as if you had used the Add Table dialog box.

4. Click the Totals button to display the Total row in the QBE grid, and in that row of the Size field, click the arrow and select Count from the drop-down list of functions.

5. Run the query. Access displays the customer number, customer name, and a count of estimates from the Size field, as shown here:

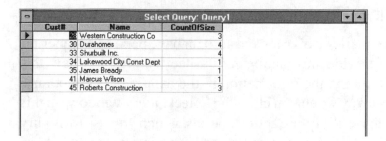

Query windows can hold several tables. For example, suppose you need to know the location, customer, size, and level of difficulty when deciding which employees to assign to new jobs. These four items of information are stored in three different tables. Here's how to extract the information:

1. Click the Design View button to switch to Design view, click the Add Table button on the toolbar, and add the Jobs table to the Select Query window.

2. Choose Clear Grid from the Edit menu to start with a fresh QBE grid.

3. Click the Totals button to remove the Total row.

4. In the Estimates box, double click the EstimateID and CustomerID fields. Then double-click the Name field in the Customers box. Next, double-click the Size and Difficulty fields in the Estimates box. And finally double-click the Location, JobID, and Status fields in the Jobs box.

5. In the Criteria row of the Status column, type *Null* to select only the jobs that have no value in the Status field. Then deselect the Status field's Show box.

6. Now run the query. The datasheet displays the requested information for two jobs (we've adjusted the column widths):

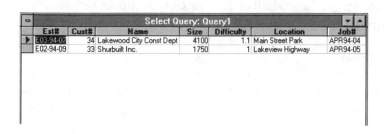

Using three tables

Relating tables

You can relate two tables that do not have a previously defined relationship in the Query window, by clicking and dragging from the linking field in the first table box to the linking field in the second table box. Access draws a line between the two fields. Remember, the fields must use the same set of values for the two tables to be related. To dissolve a relationship, click the line between the two table boxes to select it, and press the Delete key.

Action Queries

All the queries we've looked at so far have been select queries, which provide information in datasheets. Unless you save this type of query, the information in the datasheet is temporary; it goes away when you close the Select Query window. In this section, we'll explore action queries, which you use to modify the information in your tables and even to create new tables.

Updating Records

From time to time, you may want to change a field value in several records in a table. For example, if you assign a new salesperson to a sales area, you may need to change the salesperson's name in records in a customer table.

Suppose the Post Office has assigned a new ZIP code to Pinewood, and you need to update the Employees table to reflect the change. You could update each record in turn, but an easier way is to use an update query. Follow these steps:

1. To keep things simple, close any windows without saving the queries so that only the Database window is active.

2. With Employees selected in the Database window, click the New Query button on the toolbar, and then click New Query.

3. Double-click the PostalCode field to add it to the QBE grid.

Using an update query

4. Click the Update Query button on the toolbar to add an Update To row to the QBE grid.

5. In the Update To row, type *11415* in the PostalCode field.

6. In the Criteria row, type *11412* in the PostalCode field, and press Enter.

7. Run the query. Access advises you of the number of records to be updated.

8. Click OK to complete the changes.

9. Open the Employees table where the records for the two employees who live in Pinedale have been updated with the new ZIP codes.

For a small table, it may be faster to make the changes manually. For large tables, using an update query is faster and ensures that all the affected records are changed.

Creating New Tables

Earlier you used a select query to calculate the cost per 100 square feet for each item in the Materials table, and you saved the query with the name Cost. To use the calculated cost in other queries, you need to convert the datasheet produced by this query to an independent table. Here are the steps:

1. Close any open Query or Table windows without saving anything, and in the Database window, click the Query button, select Cost, and then click Open. The datasheet displays the cost per 100 square feet for each item in the Materials table.

2. Switch to Design view, and convert the select query to a make-table query by clicking the Make-Table Query button on the toolbar. Access displays this dialog box:

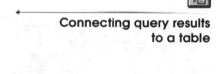

Connecting query results to a table

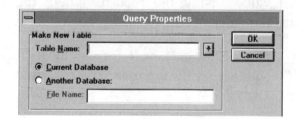

3. Type *Costs* in the Table Name edit box, and press Enter.

4. Run the query. Access asks you to confirm that you want the query results copied to a new table.

5. Click OK, and then close the Make Table Query window, clicking Yes to save the changes to the Cost query.

6. In the Database window, click the Table button. Access has added the Costs table to the Roofs database.

Performing Multi-Table Calculations

You can use mathematical formulas in multi-table queries just as you can use them in single-table queries. To demonstrate how to use formulas in an action query, let's calculate field values for the empty material and labor costs fields in the Estimates table. First you'll extract the cost of materials per 100 square feet from the Costs table you just created. You'll then use that table's information to calculate and enter material and labor costs in the Estimates table. Follow these steps:

1. Open a new query for the Costs table, which contains the cost per 100 square feet for each material.

2. Double-click first the ItemID field and then the CostPer100SF field. In the Criteria row of the ItemID field, type *F03 Or N01 Or P02 Or S02* to select the flashing, nails, paper, and shingles you will use to determine the material and labor costs.

3. Click the Totals button on the toolbar. Then in the Total row of the ItemID field, replace Group By with Where; and in the Total row of the CostPer100SF column, replace Group By with Sum.

You have told Access to perform the Sum function on the CostPer100SF field values using the records where the ItemID field contains the values F03, N01, P02, or S02.

4. Run the query. As you can see, the datasheet displays the total material cost per 100 square feet for the materials specified in the Criteria row:

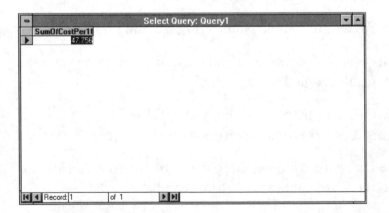

5. Having verified that the query produces the correct result, return to Design view so that you can convert the select query to a make-table query. Then click the Make-Table Query button on the toolbar, type *Standard Costs* as the new table's name in the Query Properties dialog box, and press Enter.

Crosstab queries

Crosstab queries are a useful way of displaying data in a grid format similar to a spreadsheet so that the data is easier to compare. For example, a crosstab query could be used to compare the number of estimates for each customer grouped by difficulty. To set up a crosstab query, create a new Query window for the appropriate tables, add the fields you want to see to the QBE grid, and click the Crosstab Query button to add a Crosstab row and a Total row to the QBE grid. Use the options in the Crosstab row to determine which fields are rows, columns, and values. Then set up the functions you need in the Total row, and run the query. The datasheet is displayed as a grid with the row and column headings you specified in the Crosstab row.

6. Run the query, and when Access asks you to confirm that you want to copy the results to a new table, click OK.

When estimating real jobs, a roofing company's total material cost would obviously vary depending on the type of shingles and other factors. However, for simplicity, we will use this standard material cost for all the estimates. Follow these steps to calculate the material and labor costs and fill in the empty fields in the Estimates table:

1. Close all open Query windows without saving the queries, and in the Database window, click the Query button, click New, and then click New Query. In the Add Table dialog box, double-click Standard Costs and Estimates, and then click the Close button.

Using data in one table to calculate values in another

2. Double-click the CostMaterials and CostLabor fields in the Estimates box to add them to the QBE grid, and then click the Update Query button on the toolbar.

3. Type *[SumofCostPer100SF]*([Size]/100)* in the Update To row for the CostMaterials field. This formula divides the estimate size by 100 to express the size in 100 square feet units and then multiplies the result by the cost field from the Standard Costs table. The result is the cost of materials for each estimate.

4. Type *([SumofCostPer100SF]*([Size]/100)*[Difficulty])*1.2* in the Update To row for the CostLabor field, and press Enter. This formula is a little more complex. We use the Difficulty field to adjust the labor cost based on the job difficulty, and we multiply everything by 1.2 to provide a 20% profit margin on the labor.

5. Run the query, and when Access advises you of the number of records to be changed, click OK.

6. Open the Estimates table, and adjust the column widths so that you can see the CostMaterials and CostLabor fields, which are displayed with the captions Material Cost and Labor Cost as shown on the next page.

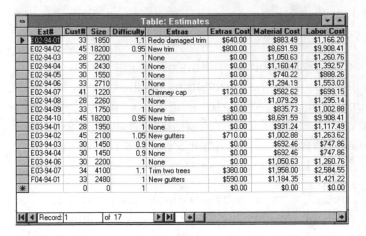

Est#	Cust#	Size	Difficulty	Extras	Extras Cost	Material Cost	Labor Cost
E02-94-01	33	1850	1.1	Redo damaged trim	$640.00	$883.49	$1,166.20
E02-94-02	45	18200	0.95	New trim	$800.00	$8,691.59	$9,908.41
E02-94-03	28	2200	1	None	$0.00	$1,050.63	$1,260.76
E02-94-04	35	2430	1	None	$0.00	$1,160.47	$1,392.57
E02-94-05	30	1550	1	None	$0.00	$740.22	$888.26
E02-94-06	33	2710	1	None	$0.00	$1,294.19	$1,553.03
E02-94-07	41	1220	1	Chimney cap	$120.00	$582.62	$699.15
E02-94-08	28	2260	1	None	$0.00	$1,079.29	$1,295.14
E02-94-09	33	1750	1	None	$0.00	$835.73	$1,002.88
E02-94-10	45	18200	0.95	New trim	$800.00	$8,691.59	$9,908.41
E03-94-01	28	1950	1	None	$0.00	$931.24	$1,117.49
E03-94-02	45	2100	1.05	New gutters	$710.00	$1,002.88	$1,263.62
E03-94-03	30	1450	0.9	None	$0.00	$692.46	$747.86
E03-94-04	30	1450	0.9	None	$0.00	$692.46	$747.86
E03-94-06	30	2200	1	None	$0.00	$1,050.63	$1,260.76
E03-94-07	34	4100	1.1	Trim two trees	$380.00	$1,958.00	$2,584.55
F04-94-01	33	2480	1	New gutters	$590.00	$1,184.35	$1,421.22
*	0	0	1		$0.00	$0.00	$0.00

Error messages

If running the query produces an error message, check the formulas in the Update To row. A missing or backwards bracket or parenthesis may be all that's holding things up.

These formulas are complex, but if you analyze them carefully, their logic will be clear and you will easily be able to create similar formulas to meet your own needs. The complexity of the formulas you use in your queries is often limited only by your own creativity. If you aren't sure of the outcome of a query, make copies of your tables and test the query on the copies before running it on the actual tables. (Page 36 has the steps for copying tables.)

Moving Records

The data you keep in tables is rarely static. You will often find it easier to work with data that is relevant for the present in one table and then move the data to another table for archiving. The roofing company's Jobs table is a good example. If you keep all the jobs the company has ever worked on in one table, the table will soon become too large to work with on a daily basis. The solution is to have a separate table for the records of jobs that are finished.

To set the stage for the next example, you need to change the Status field values of two records in the Jobs table to *Closed*, indicating not only that the work is complete but that payment has been received. You also need to create a new table to contain the records for closed jobs. Let's get going:

SQL-based queries

Those of you who have programming experience might want to experiment with three types of queries that consist of SQL (*structured query language*) statements: union, pass-through, and data-definition queries. Union queries combine fields from two or more tables; pass-through queries let you pass commands through to an SQL database, and data-definition queries let you create, modify, and delete Access tables. If you want to take a look at some SQL statements, open a query in Datasheet or Design view, and click the SQL button on the toolbar. The statements underlying the query then appear in a window.

1. To keep your desktop neat, close any Query and Table windows without saving them. Then open the Jobs table, change the Status values for the records with job numbers MAR94-01 and MAR94-03 to *Closed*, and close the table, saving the changes.

2. With Jobs highlighted in the Database window, click the Copy button on the toolbar.

3. Now click the Paste button on the toolbar, and in the Paste Table As dialog box, name the table *Closed Jobs*, click Structure Only, and then click OK. Access adds the new table to the list in the Database window.

4. Open the Closed Jobs table in Design view, and delete the Status field by clicking its row selector and pressing Delete.

5. Close the table, saving the changes when prompted.

You are now ready to move the closed records from the Jobs table to the Closed Jobs table. This is a two-step, append-and-delete operation.

Appending Records

We now have a table in which to store the records for the jobs that are closed. Follow these steps to move the closed jobs to the Closed Jobs table:

1. Select the Jobs table in the Database window, click the New Query button on the toolbar, and then click New Query.

Archiving records

2. Add all the fields from the Jobs box to the QBE grid by double-clicking the Jobs title bar and dragging the pointer to the grid.

3. Type *Closed* in the Criteria row of the Status field.

4. Now click the Append Query button on the toolbar, and when Access displays the Query Properties dialog box, type *Closed Jobs* as the name of the table to which you want to append the results of the query, and then click OK.

5. Run the query, and when Access advises you that it will append two rows, click OK to proceed with the query.

6. Close the Append Query window, saving the query as *Append Closed Jobs*.

7. Open the Closed Jobs table to verify that it contains the two closed records, as shown here:

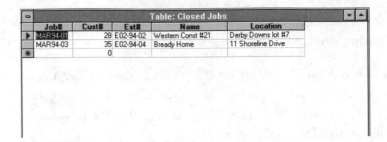

Because you saved the query, it will be listed in the query list in the Database window, so you can run it when you need to append records from the Jobs table to the Closed Jobs table.

Deleting Records

You have copied the closed records to the Closed Jobs table, but the records still exist in the Jobs table. You could easily delete them individually because there are only two. But what if you want to delete a large number of records that are scattered throughout the table? A better technique is to set up a query to delete the records for you. Follow these steps:

1. Close any Query and Table windows, and open a new query for the Jobs table.

2. Add all the fields in the Jobs box to the QBE grid, and in the Criteria row of the Status field, type *Closed*.

3. Click the Delete Query button on the toolbar. Access adds a row to the QBE grid with Where in each field.

4. Without changing any of the entries in the grid, run the query. When Access advises you that two records will be deleted, click OK. Access then displays this message:

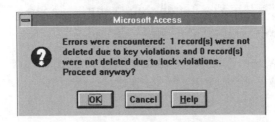

The results demonstrate how Access safeguards your databases by preventing you from introducing errors. Access does not tell you exactly what the problem is, but it does tell you that deleting one or both of the records will produce key violations, meaning that the record or records are referenced by at least one record in a related table. Let's do a little sleuthing:

Error prevention

1. Click Cancel, and activate the Database window.

Tracking the source of errors

2. With Jobs selected in the list of tables, click the Relationships button on the toolbar to display the relationships you've established between the tables of the Roofs database. As you can see, the Employees table references the JobID field of the Jobs table. If you check the job assignments of the employees, you'll see that an employee is still assigned to job number MAR94-01, even though it is closed. You need to change the field value in the Employees table before you can delete the closed job record from the Jobs table. Here are the steps:

3. Close the Relationships window, and then open the Employees table.

4. Click anywhere in the Job# column, click the Find button on the toobar, type *MAR94-01* in the Find What edit box, click Find Next, and then click Close. Access locates MAR94-01 in the record for Ron Westerman.

5. Ron should be assigned to job number APR94-02, so make this change, and then close the Employees table.

6. Activate the Delete Query window for the Jobs table, and rerun the query. When you click OK, Access deletes the two closed records.

7. Close the Query window, saving the query as *Delete Closed Jobs*.

As you have seen, queries allow you to selectively view or modify the data from one or more tables. In the next two chapters, we'll also show you how to select information for display in a form or report.

4

Using Forms to View
and Manipulate Data

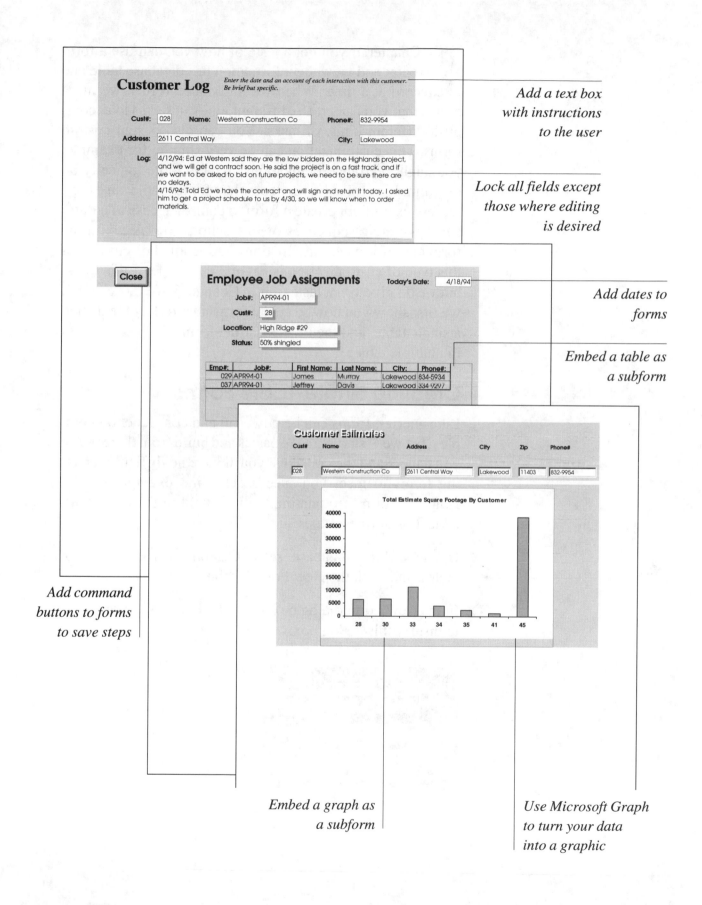

Customer Log

Enter the date and an account of each interaction with this customer. Be brief but specific.

Cust#: 028   Name: Western Construction Co   Phone#: 832-9954

Address: 2611 Central Way   City: Lakewood

Log: 4/12/94: Ed at Western said they are the low bidders on the Highlands project, and we will get a contract soon. He said the project is on a fast track, and if we want to be asked to bid on future projects, we need to be sure there are no delays.
4/15/94: Told Ed we have the contract and will sign and return it today. I asked him to get a project schedule to us by 4/30, so we will know when to order materials.

Add a text box with instructions to the user

Lock all fields except those where editing is desired

Close

Employee Job Assignments   Today's Date: 4/18/94

Job#: APR94-01

Cust#: 28

Location: High Ridge #29

Status: 50% shingled

Add dates to forms

Embed a table as a subform

Emp#:	Job#:	First Name:	Last Name:	City:	Phone#:
029	APR94-01	James	Murray	Lakewood	834-5934
037	APR94-01	Jeffrey	Davis	Lakewood	334-9297

Customer Estimates

Cust#	Name	Address	City	Zip	Phone#
028	Western Construction Co	2611 Central Way	Lakewood	11403	832-9954

Total Estimate Square Footage By Customer

Add command buttons to forms to save steps

Embed a graph as a subform

Use Microsoft Graph to turn your data into a graphic

In Chapter 1, you got a taste of how you can use a form to enter and view the information in a database table one record at a time. When we introduced forms, we mentioned that you can create different kinds of forms to accomplish different kinds of tasks. You can also design custom forms. This customization can be very simple; for example, you might rearrange fields to group them more logically on the form. It can also be very complex; for example, an expert Access user might create a form to control access to a database, assigning sequences of instructions to objects on the form to perform certain functions. (A detailed discussion of this type of customization is beyond the scope of this book, but we do give you a taste of it in Chapter 6.) In this chapter, we first show you how to create forms that reflect the data in a single table, and then we construct forms that use the data in multiple tables.

Creating Single-Table Forms

Like queries, forms can be powerful and consequently complex, but we'll start with the basics and build from there. Once you understand the concepts, you'll have no difficulty creating forms to meet your needs. The first example is very simple: a form for updating the Log field in the Customers table. Follow these steps:

1. Open the Roofs database, select Customers from the list of tables, and click the New Form button on the toolbar.

2. In the New Form dialog box, click the Form Wizards button to display this dialog box:

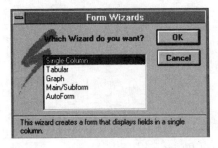

3. Accept the default Single-Column format by clicking OK. Access displays the first of a series of Single-Column Form Wizard dialog boxes:

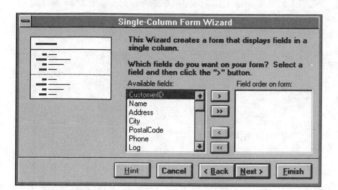

4. With CustomerID selected in the Available Fields list, click the > button to move that field name to the list on the right.

Entering fields in forms

5. Repeat step 4 for the Name, Phone, and Log fields, and then click the Next button to display this dialog box:

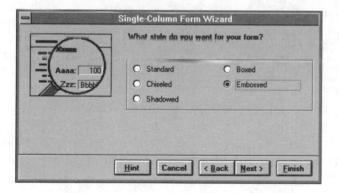

6. Click Standard, and click Next to display the last dialog box:

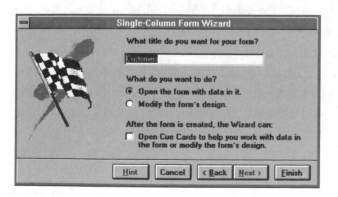

Creating forms from scratch

You can create a blank form by clicking the Form button in the Database window, clicking New, and then clicking Blank Form in the New Form dialog box. Access switches to Design view and displays a form containing only the Detail section, ready for you to add the controls you want. To add a Form Header and Footer or a Page Header and Footer, choose the corresponding command from the Format menu.

7. Click Modify The Form's Design, and then click Finish to display this Form window:

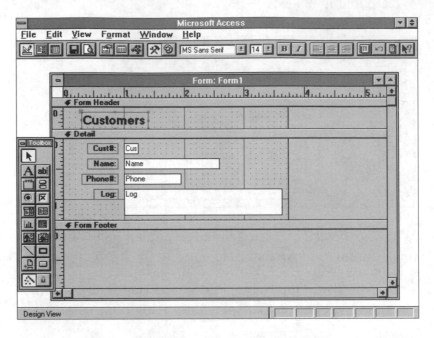

We have hidden the Database window behind the Form window to avoid screen clutter; you might want to do the same.

8. Save the form by clicking the Save button on the toolbar, typing *Customer Log* as the form's name in the Save As dialog box, and pressing Enter. The form's name is now displayed in the window's title bar.

The Form window

The Form window is divided into three sections: the Form Header, which currently displays the name of the table on which the form is based at the top of the form; the Detail section, which displays white boxes called *controls* and gray boxes called *labels* for each of the fields you selected for inclusion in the form; and the Form Footer, which, like the Form Header, can contain information such as a title or date that you want to appear at the bottom of the form. Two other sections, Page Header and Page Footer, are not visible in the form now on your screen. They contain elements you want to appear on every page of a multi-page form. The window also contains horizontal and vertical rulers and gridlines that help you position controls on the form.

Controls and labels

Customizing Forms

You have created a new form, but you haven't yet used any of the features that make forms unique. Let's edit the Customer Log form to include some of these features:

1. First, click the Control menu icon at the left end of the title bar of the Toolbox displayed on the left side of your screen. You'll use some of these tools later, but for now turning off the Toolbox (and any other tools) will reduce screen clutter.

2. Click the Name control. Small squares, called *handles*, appear around the control's border.

   Rearranging controls

3. Point to the selected control, and when the pointer changes to a small open hand, drag the control and its label to the right of the CustomerID control (shown as *Cus*). Use the rulers to help align the controls, and if necessary, enlarge the Detail section.

4. Next select and drag the Phone control and its label to the right of the Name control.

5. Because the whole purpose of this form is to make it easy to maintain customer logs, it would help if the Log control really stood out on the form. Select the Log control, and move it and its label up under the three rearranged controls. Then point to the handle in the bottom right corner of the control, and when the pointer changes to a diagonal double-headed arrow, drag down and to the right to enlarge the control. Access adjusts the size of the Form Footer area to accommodate the new control size, and the form now looks like this:

   Enlarging controls

> **Two types of hands**
>
> To move a control and its label on a form so that they maintain their relative positions, select the control and drag the black open hand that appears when you point to the control's border. To move a control independently of its label, select the control and drag the black pointing hand that appears when you point to the large handle in the control's top left corner. Similarly, to move a label independently, select the label and drag the pointing hand.

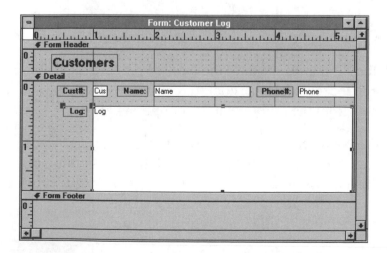

Now let's change the color of some of the controls:

1. Click the Palette button on the toolbar to display a palette of colors that you can apply to the characters (Fore), background (Back), and border of your controls.

2. Click the Cus control, and select a bright color in the Back row of the palette.

3. Repeat step 2 for the Name and Phone controls, using different colors.

4. Click the palette's Control menu icon to remove the palette from the screen.

You want to ensure that only the Log control can be changed through this form, so you need to make the other controls *read only* by locking them. Here are the steps for making this change:

1. Click the Cus control, and then click the Properties button on the toolbar to display this list of customizable properties:

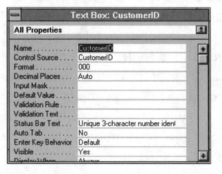

Text Box: CustomerID	
All Properties	
Name	CustomerID
Control Source	CustomerID
Format	000
Decimal Places . . .	Auto
Input Mask	
Default Value	
Validation Rule	
Validation Text	
Status Bar Text . . .	Unique 3-character number idenl
Auto Tab	No
Enter Key Behavior	Default
Visible	Yes
Display When	Always

You might want to take a minute to scroll through the list to see the properties you can set from this window.

2. Scroll the Properties list until the Locked property is visible, click the Locked edit box, click the arrow to the right, and select Yes from the drop-down list of options.

3. Click the Name control in the form (if necessary, move the Properties window out of the way by dragging its title bar), and then repeat step 2. Do the same for the Phone control. Then double-click the Control menu icon at the left end of the Properties window's title bar to close the window.

Formatting control borders

The Palette provides buttons you can click to change the appearance of your controls. You can change their general look to make them seem embossed or pressed, and you can customize their borders by changing their thickness, type, and color. You can even specify which sides of a control should have borders.

4. Next, click the Save button to save the changes to the form.

5. Click the Form View button on the toolbar to display the form in Form view, as shown here:

Switching to Form view

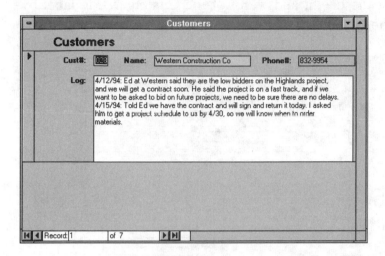

Now anyone can update the Log field without risk of a wrong keystroke deleting a record or changing information in another field.

Editing the Form's Title

The Form Header section currently displays the name of the table on which this form is based as the form's title. Sometimes this information will be all you need in the Form window to orient the form's users. But often you will want to edit the title to spell out the purpose of the form. To edit the title, follow these steps:

1. Switch to Design view, click the Customers label in the Form Header section, and click an insertion point after the last *s*.

2. Press Backspace, and then type a space and the word *Log*.

3. Click anywhere outside the label to admire your work. Then click the label to select it again, and click the Properties button to display the list of customizable properties.

Formatting the form's title

4. Scroll the options, click the Font Name edit box, click the arrow, and select Times New Roman.

5. Replace 14 in the Font Size edit box with 18.

6. Click the Font Weight edit box, click the arrow, select Heavy from the bottom of the list of options, and then double-click the window's Control menu icon to close the window.

7. Adjust the height and width of the Customer Log label by dragging its handles until the entire title is visible, like this:

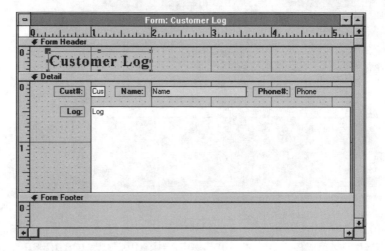

Adding Other Elements

Now let's see what else we can do to customize the form. In this section, we'll use some of the tools in the Toolbox to add more controls to facilitate the form's use.

Adding Text

Suppose you want to add instructions to the Form Header section to further explain the purpose of this form. Using the Label tool, you can add any text you feel would be helpful. Try this:

1. First click the Toolbox button on the toolbar to display the Toolbox.

2. Click the Label tool, position the cross-hair pointer in the Form Header section slightly to the right of the Customer Log label's top right corner, and drag a new box the height and width of the remaining Form Header section.

3. Type *Enter the date and an account of each interaction with this customer. Be brief but specific.*

4. Click anywhere outside the label, and then click the label to select it.

5. On the toolbar, click the arrow to the right of the font name (MS Sans Serif) to drop down a list of fonts, and select Times New Roman from the bottom of the list. Then click the Bold button to turn off the bold style, and click the Italic button to turn on the italic style. Finally, change from right to left alignment by clicking the Left Align button.

6. Click the Form View button to see these results:

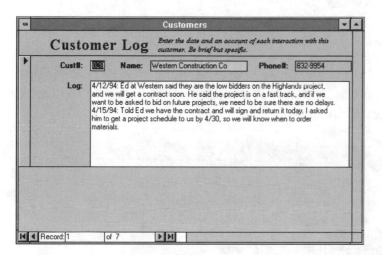

Adding Command Buttons

Access allows you to place objects called *command buttons* on a form so that you can simply click the button to carry out a particular task. The task is actually accomplished by a set of instructions called a *macro* that is attached to the button. As an example, we'll create a "close" button in the Form Footer section that you can click to close the Form window. The following steps show you how to use a wizard to create the button:

Macros

1. Click the Design View button to switch the Customer Log form to Design view, and if it is not already active ("pressed"), click the Control Wizards tool at the bottom of the Toolbox.

2. Click the Command Button tool in the Toolbox, position the pointer on the left side of the Form Footer section, hold down the mouse button, and drag to create a box about 3/4 inch long and 1/4 inch high. When you release the mouse button,

Access turns the box into a button and displays the first
Command Button Wizard dialog box:

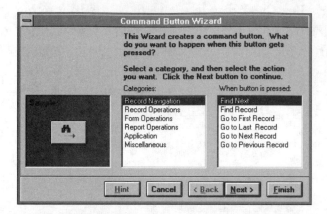

**Assigning actions to
command buttons**

3. Select Form Operations in the Categories list and Close Form
in the When Button Is Pressed list, and click Next to display
the second dialog box:

Assigning the button's label

4. Click the Text option, delete the word *Form* from the adjacent
edit box, and click Next to display this dialog box:

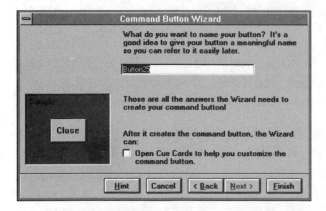

5. In the last dialog box, type *FormClose* as the name of the button, and click Finish. Here's the result:

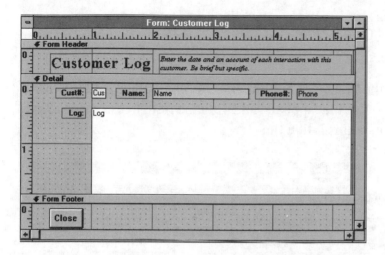

6. Click the Save button to save the changes to the form.

Now for the acid test. Let's try out the new button:

1. Click the Form View button on the toolbar to switch the form to Form view.

2. Click the new Close button, and if necessary, click Yes to save any outstanding changes.

The ability to create buttons to perform routine operations really enhances what you can do with forms. But you are not limited to the operations provided by the Command Button Wizard. If you repeatedly need to carry out cumbersome or complicated database operations, there is a good possibility that you can simplify your work by writing your own macros and attaching them to buttons. Chapter 6 gives a few more examples of what you can do with macros, and we also encourage those of you who are interested to explore the topic further in the documentation.

Adding Controls

When you created the Customer Log form, you didn't include a control for the Address field. Suppose you decide you need that control in the form. Follow the steps on the next page.

Selecting button icons

Clicking the Show All Pictures option in the second Command Button Wizard dialog box displays a list of available button icons. You can scroll through the list, highlighting different icon names to see the corresponding icon displayed in the sample box to the left. Or you can click the Browse button to display the Select Bitmap dialog box, which enables you to locate the graphic you want to use as your button's icon.

1. With the Customer Log form selected in the Database window, click the Design button.

2. In the Detail section, select the Log control, and move it and its label down so that there is room above them for another control.

3. Click the Field List button on the toolbar, click Address in the list of fields that appears, and drag the field to the space above the Log control, like this:

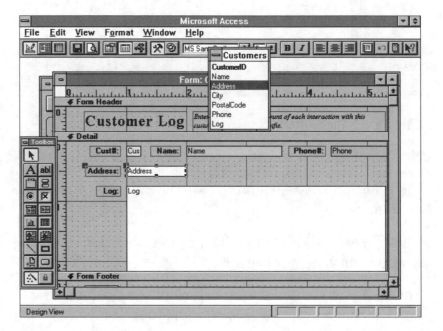

4. Enlarge the Address control so that it can hold a complete street address (see page 97).

5. Close the Field List box.

Adding a Drop-Down List of Options

Forms are often used to provide access to tables in a simple, controlled environment, and you can even create drop-down lists and check boxes to present a limited set of options to the form's users. Follow these steps to assign a drop-down list to the City control:

1. Click the Combo Box tool in the Toolbox. (If you closed the Toolbox, click the Toolbox button on the toolbar to open it.)

2. Click the Field List button on the toolbar.

3. Click the City field, and drag it onto the form below the Phone control. (You might need to position the label and the control separately once you have them on the form.) Access displays the first Combo Box Wizard dialog box:

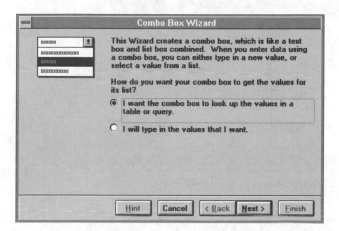

4. Click the I Will Type... option, and then click Next to display the second dialog box:

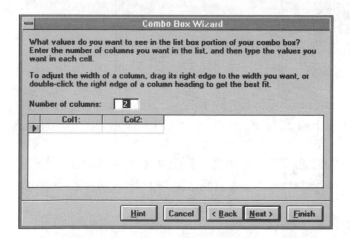

5. Type *1* as the number of columns. Then click the Col1 edit box, type *Lakewood*, press Enter, type *Pinedale*, press Enter again, and type *Falls City*. Then click Next to display the third Combo Box Wizard dialog box shown on the next page.

Handy helpers

To save time as you work on the design of a form, you can open the Properties window, Toolbox, and Field List window and leave them open while you switch between Form view and Design view. All three of these tools disappear but stay active when you switch to Form view and then reappear as soon as you switch back to Design view.

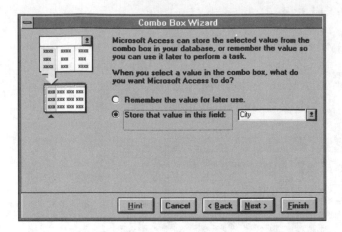

6. Click the Store That Value... option, and click Next.

Adding a group of option buttons

To add a group of buttons for mutually exclusive options to a form, start by clicking the Option Group tool in the Toolbox. In the first Wizard dialog box, list the options in the group. Then indicate whether one option is the default and if so, which one. Next, specify the values to be assigned to each option for storage purposes and where you want the value stored. Then specify how the buttons should look on the form, and assign them a group name. On the form, the buttons appear surrounded by a group box, and only one of them can be selected at a time.

7. Click the Finish button to return to your form, and then scroll the form to see the new City control with its drop-down arrow:

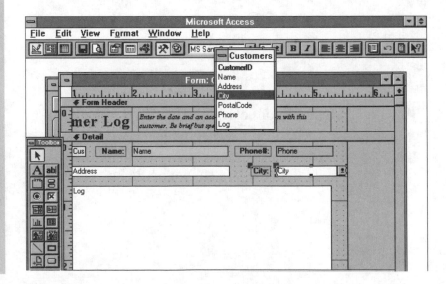

8. Close the Field List box, and then click the Form View button on the toolbar to see the results. The City control contains the field value for the current record. If you were entering the record for a new customer, you could click the arrow to see a list of possible values for the City control. You could also type a City value, but when only a few values are likely, using a drop-down list helps keep field values consistent.

9. Click anywhere on the form to close the drop-down list, and then close the form, saving your changes.

The Toolbox provides many tools with which you can customize forms. For practice, you might want to add other elements to the Customer Log form. If you need help, click the Help button, point to the tool you want to know more about, and click. Double-click the Help window's Control menu icon to return to the Form window.

Help with Toolbox tools

Creating Multi-Table Forms

You now have a basic understanding of how to create and customize forms. With that foundation, let's move on to see why forms are such powerful tools. As you know, forms are a useful way of entering or editing data in a table, but you can also use forms to view, add, or edit data in multiple tables.

When you create a form with two or more tables, you can take advantage of any existing relationships. For example, when you created the Jobs table, you designated the JobID field as the primary key field. (You'll recall that all the values in a primary key field must be unique.) In the Employees table, you created a JobID field to establish a relationship between the two tables; in the Employees table, the JobID field is a foreign key.

Table relationships and forms

The relationship between the Jobs and Employees tables is one-to-many—one job can have many employees assigned to it. You can also create one-to-one relationships—only one record in the first table matches only one record in the second table. You might create a one-to-one relationship between a table that contains employee payroll information and a table that contains employee personal information. The employee number is the key field in both tables, and each employee has only one record in each table.

Aligning controls

You can use the Align command on the Format menu to left-align, right-align, top-align, or bottom-align the controls in your forms. First select the control or controls you want to align (hold down the Shift key and click each control to select an entire group). Then choose Align from the Format menu and one of the commands from the submenu. You can also align the controls to the nearest gridline by choosing Align and then To Grid.

As an example, let's use the Jobs and Employees tables to create a form for assigning employees to different jobs. Follow these steps:

1. Close any open windows without saving, and with Jobs selected in the list of tables in the Database window, click the New Form button on the toolbar. Then click Form Wizards in the New Form dialog box.

2. Select Main/Subform, and click OK. Access displays the first Main/Subform Wizard dialog box:

3. Select Employees as the subform table, and click Next. Access asks you to select the fields for the main form.

4. Add the JobID, CustomerID, Location, and Status fields to the main form from the Jobs table, and then click Next. Now Access asks you to select the fields for the subform.

5. Add the EmployeeID, JobID, FirstName, LastName, City, and HomePhone fields to the subform, and click Next.

6. In the fourth dialog box, select Shadowed as the form's style, and click Next.

7. Now type *Employee Job Assignments* as the title that will appear in the Form Header section of the form, and click Finish.

8. Access prompts you to save the subform. Click OK to close the message box, name the subform *Employees*, and press Enter. Access displays the form in a Form window:

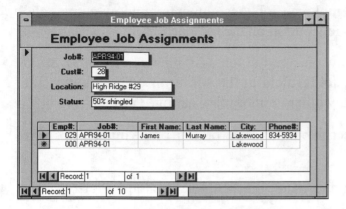

As you can see, the main form displays information for job APR94-01, and the subform displays information about employees assigned to that job. Clicking the Next Record button at the bottom of the window displays information about the next job in the Jobs table, and the subform records change to display information about the employees assigned to that job.

Moving among records

As the form is now, any of the information in either the main form or the subform can be edited. You need to lock all the controls except for JobID in the subform so that only that field can be edited in the Form window. Follow these steps to lock the controls of the main form:

1. Click the Design View button on the toolbar.

Locking controls in the main form

2. Click the JobID control in the main form to select it, click the Properties button on the toolbar, and in the Properties window, change the Locked property to Yes.

3. Without closing the Properties window, repeat step 2 for the CustomerID, Location, and Status controls.

Because the subform is a separate form, you need to open that form in Design view to lock its controls. Follow these steps:

1. Double-click the Employees subform control. Access opens the Employees form in Design view.

Locking controls in the subform

2. Change the Locked property of all the controls except JobID to Yes.

3. Close the Properties window, and then close the Employees window, saving the changes to the Employees form when prompted.

4. With the Employee Job Assignments window active, click the Form View button on the toolbar.

You can now change the job assignments of employees by editing the JobID field in the subform, without any risk of changing any other item of information. Try this:

Editing fields in the subform

1. Using the scroll buttons at the bottom of the main form, move to record 3.

2. In the subform, change the JobID field value for Jeffrey Davis to APR94-01.

3. Scroll back to record 1. Note that Jeffrey Davis is now assigned to job number APR94-01.

4. Close the form, saving it as *Employee Job Assignments*.

Establishing relationships while creating forms

Creating a form is an easy way to show data from several tables or queries while limiting access to the data. But what if the relationships you want to use between two or more tables in a form have not been established yet? You can still use the tables when you create the form because Access will establish a relationship if the appropriate fields exist in the tables. If Access cannot intuit which fields are related, you can specify which fields the program should use to link the subform and main form.

Adding a Subform

Let's add a subform, based on the Customers table, to the Employee Job Assignments form so that information about each customer is close at hand:

1. With the Customers table selected in the Database window, click the New Form button on the toolbar, and use the Form Wizards to create a standard, single-column form that displays only the customer's name and phone number. Finish by opening the new form in Design view.

Removing the Form Header and Footer

2. Choose Form Header/Footer from the Format menu to remove those sections from the form. Click OK when asked to confirm this action.

3. Close the Form window, saving the form as *Customers*.

4. Click Form in the Database window, and open the Employee Job Assignments form in Design view. If the Toolbox is not displayed, open it by clicking Toolbox on the toolbar.

5. Click the Subform/Subreport tool in the Toolbox, and create a subform area to the right of the Jobs controls. The subform appears in your form as an unbound box, like this:

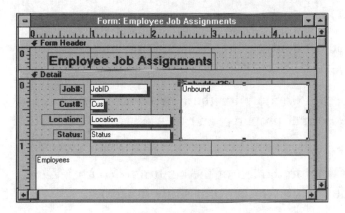

6. To assign a table to the unbound box, open its Properties window, click the Source Object edit box, click the arrow, and select Customers.

7. Type *CustomerID* in both the Link Child Fields and Link Master Fields edit boxes.

8. Change the Visible property from Yes to No, close the Properties window, and click the Form View button on the toolbar.

You have added customer information to the Employee Job Assignments form without creating unnecessary clutter. If you don't recognize a customer number, you can switch the Visible property back to Yes to display the customer's name and phone number. The ability to create a relationship between the Customers form and the Employee Job Assignments form is a result of the way you designed the database. You anticipated the possibility of needing to see related information from different tables and created the fields that allow you to bring the information together.

Adding the Date

With controls, you can display all sorts of information in a form, some of it from tables or queries, and some from other

Bound vs. unbound controls

A bound control is linked to a field in a table. You use bound controls to display and enter field values. An unbound control isn't linked to another database element unless you establish the link. You can use unbound controls to display information that is not in your tables, such as instructions to the user, or you can establish a link to an existing database element through the Source Object property in the Properties window.

Creating a text-box control

sources. For example, you can display the current date in the Employee Job Assignments form by following these steps:

1. Switch to Design view, click the Text Box tool in the Toolbox, and create a text-box control to the right of the title in the Form Header section.

2. Click in the new control (the word *Unbound* disappears), and type *=Date()*.

3. Click outside the control, and then click the control again to select it.

4. In the Properties window for the new control, select Short Date as the Format property, and then close the Properties window.

5. Change the label to the left of the control to *Today's Date:*, adjusting the position of the form's title if necessary.

6. Switch to Form view to see these results:

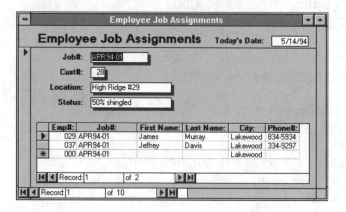

Adding the time and page numbers

You can also create controls to show the time (*=Time()*), page number (*=Page()*).

Adding Calculated Controls

Suppose you want to create a form that will display the bid amount for each job. In addition, you want to calculate the cost of preparing the estimate using a rate of 5 cents per square foot. Follow these steps to create a form based on the Estimates table that contains two calculated controls:

1. Close any open windows, and use the Form Wizards to create a standard, single-column form based on the Estimates table. Display the EstimateID, Size, Difficulty, CostExtras, Cost-Materials, and CostLabor fields, type *Estimate Size* as the form's title, and open the form in Design view.

2. Display the Properties window for the CostExtras control, and change its Visible property to No. Repeat this step for the CostMaterials and CostLabor controls. (Although the controls are still visible in Design view, they will not be displayed in Form view.)

3. Select all the controls by clicking the first one, holding down the Shift key, and then clicking each of the others in turn. Then make all the controls equal in width by choosing Size and then To Widest from the Format menu.

Selecting multiple controls

Equalizing control size

4. Choose Save As from the File menu, and save the form as *Estimate Size*.

Now let's add the calculated controls:

1. Choose Form Header/Footer from the Format menu to turn off those sections, confirming the deletion of any controls by clicking OK.

2. Point to the bottom border of the Detail section, and drag down to enlarge the section. Then drag the three cost controls to the bottom of the section, where they will be out of the way.

3. Click the Text Box tool in the Toolbox, and add an unbound control about 3 inches wide below the Difficulty control.

4. Change the label of the control to *Bid*.

5. Display the Properties window for the new control, click the Control Source edit box, and then click the Build button to the right to display the Expression Builder dialog box. Click the = button. Then with Estimate Size selected in the list on the left, double-click CostExtras in the middle box, click the + button, double-click CostMaterials, click +, and double-click CostLabor. The dialog box now looks like the one on the next page.

Duplicating fields

To copy a control to another part of the same form, select the control and choose Duplicate from the Edit menu. Access creates an exact copy of the control and you can then move it into position. You can also cut, or copy, and paste a control from one form to another using the Cut, Copy, and Paste commands on the Edit menu.

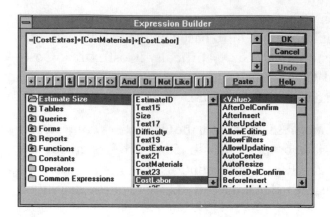

6. Now click OK to transfer the formula to the Control Source edit box.

7. Click the Format edit box, click the arrow, and select Currency. Then close the Properties window.

8. Create another text-box control below the first one, change its label to *Estimate Cost*, and in its Properties window, type =[Size]*0.05 in the Control Source edit box, and change the Format property to Currency.

9. Switch to Form view to see these results:

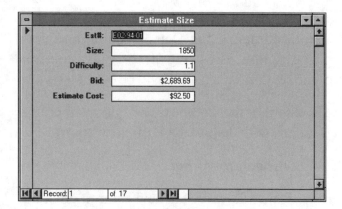

Continuous forms

The Properties window for the entire form has many useful properties, one of which is Default View. This property offers three ways to view the form: Single Form, Continuous Forms, and Datasheet. The default is the single form view. If you set the Default View property to Continuous Forms and then switch to Form view, you see the fields that have controls in the Detail section repeated for each record in the database. If you set the property to Datasheet, Access shows the form's information in a datasheet.

Access displays the first estimate and the cost of preparing the estimate. This information will be more useful if you add it to another form identifying the customer. Follow these steps to create a main form based on the Customers table:

1. Close the Estimate Size form, saving the changes you have made when prompted.

2. Create a new, standard single-column form for the Customers table using only the Name field. Type *Estimate By Customer* as the form's title, and open the form in Design view.

3. Enlarge the Detail section of the form to accommodate the Estimate Size form.

4. Click the Subform/Subreport tool in the Toolbox, and create a subform below the Name control. Select the new unbound control's label, and remove it by pressing Delete. Select the control, open its Properties window, and then select the Estimate Size form as the Source Object.

5. Now switch to Form view. Here's the new form:

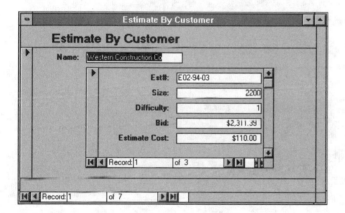

You can scroll through the customer records using the scroll buttons at the bottom of the window and scroll through the estimates for each customer using the scroll buttons at the bottom of the subform.

6. Close the form, saving it as *Estimate By Customer*.

Using Graphs in Forms

Graphs are sometimes the most logical way to present data because they allow people to quickly make visual comparisons. Creating a basic graph in Access is as simple as walking through a series of Form Wizards dialog boxes. You can then customize the graph in Design view using the Microsoft Graph application.

Let's start by creating a graph based on the Estimates table. Follow the steps on the next page.

Using the Grid commands

If you need help aligning the controls in your form, you can display a grid by choosing the Grid command from the View menu. (This command is turned on by default.) You can then use the Snap To Grid, Align To Grid, and Size To Grid commands on the Format menu to place and size the controls within the grid. If you don't see gridlines when you choose the Grid command from the View menu, open the Properties window for the form, and check the Grid X and Grid Y values, which control the number of gridlines per inch. If these values are too large, the grid may be too fine to display. Try changing the values to 10 or 12.

1. In the Database window, select the Estimates table as the data source, click the New Form button on the toolbar, click Form Wizards, and then double-click Graph to display this Graph Wizard dialog box:

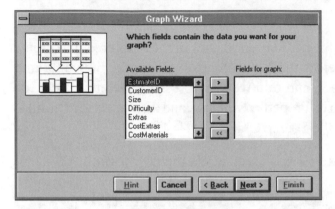

2. Select CustomerID and Size as the fields for the graph, and click Next to display the second dialog box:

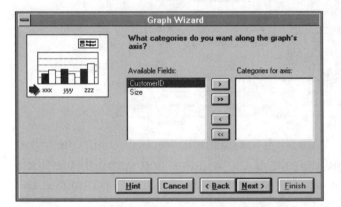

The category (X) and value (Y) axes

The category axis (often called the X axis) plots your data series, which are items such as products, or registered voters, or the departments in a large company. The value axis (often called the Y axis) compares a particular value associated with the items, such as the quantity of various products sold in the month of June, or the number of people who have voted in a particular state in each of the last ten general elections, or the number of dollars in each department's annual budget.

3. Select the CustomerID field as the one that will supply labels for the category (X) axis, and click Next.

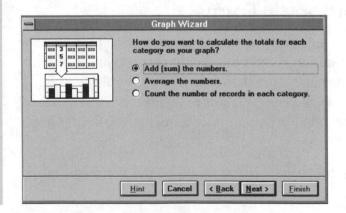

4. Click Next to specify that you want the values in the Size field totaled for each value in the CustomerID field.

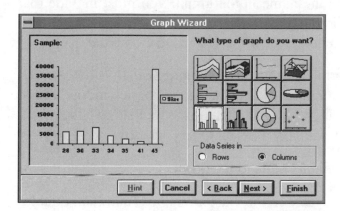

5. Click Next to tell Access to plot your data as a simple column chart. The fifth Graph Wizard dialog box appears:

Specifying the type of graph

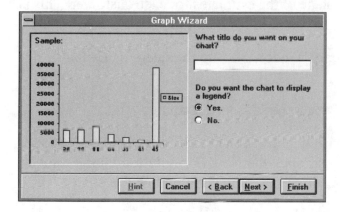

6. Assign the title *Total Estimate Square Footage By Customer*, click No to indicate that you don't want a legend, and click Next and then Finish. Here is the graph:

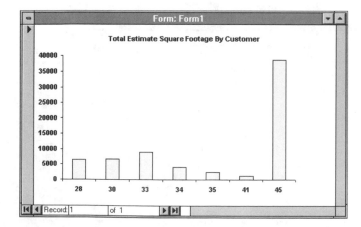

The graph is pretty but not very informative. One problem is that it displays only the customer number, not the customer name. To see the name in the graph, you must include that information in the data source by basing the data source on a multi-table query. Follow these steps to create the query:

Basing a graph on a query

1. Close the form, saving it as *Estimate Size By CustomerID*. Then with Estimates selected in the Database window's table list, click the New Query button on the toolbar, and then click New Query to display a Select Query window.

2. Add the Customers table to the query.

3. Double-click Name in the Customers box, and then double-click Size in the Estimates box.

4. Run the query to see the results. The query datasheet shows the square footage of the estimates for each customer. This is the information you need for the graph.

5. Close the Query window, saving the query as *Estimate Size By Customer*.

Now let's have another go at the graph:

1. In the Database window, select Estimate Size By Customer in the query list, click the New Form button on the toolbar, click Form Wizards, and then double-click Graph.

2. Display both the Name and Size fields on the graph, total (sum) the sizes, accept the default graph type, assign *Total Estimate Square Footage By Customer* as the title, don't display a legend, and then open this form in Form view:

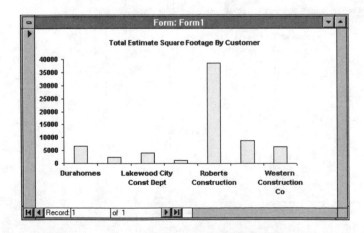

Because the query has one text field and one numeric field, Access assumed you wanted to plot the numeric data and used the text values as labels for the category (X) axis.

3. Choose Save Form As from the File menu, and save the form as *Estimate Size By Customer*.

The new graph displays the customer names and the total square footage for all their estimates. Some elements, such as the customer names, need formatting changes to make them look better. You can easily spruce up the graph by switching to Design view and opening the Microsoft Graph program that comes with Access. Follow these steps:

1. Click the Design View button on the toolbar, and double-click anywhere on the graph itself to start Microsoft Graph. If necessary, click the Chart window so that you can see the graph, like this:

Opening Microsoft Graph

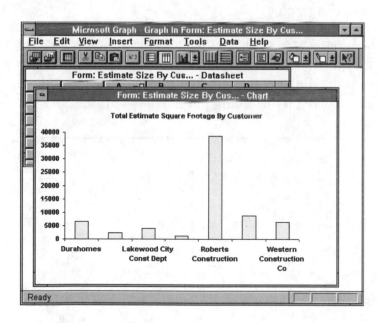

The graph is now displayed in a Chart window with the information on which the graph is based in a Datasheet window in the background.

2. Click the category (X) axis—the horizontal 0 line—choose Selected Axis from the Format menu, and click the Alignment tab. Select the sideways bottom-to-top orientation, and then click OK. Then resize the Chart window so that the axis labels

Reorienting axis labels

(the customer names) are spaced evenly and broken logically, as shown here:

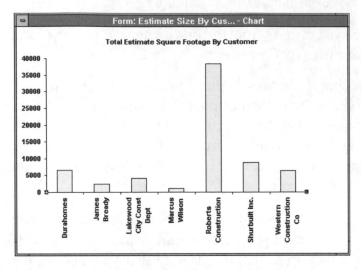

Adding gridlines

Changing the chart type

3. Click the Horizontal Gridlines button on the toolbar to add gridlines to the graph.

4. Click the Chart Type button on the toolbar, and select the 3-D Column type (the third one down on the right) from the drop-down list. Enlarge the window as necessary to produce the results shown on the facing page.

Types of graphs

Listed here is a summary of the types of graphs you can create in Access. The type of graph you select depends on the kind of data you want to display.

Bar graphs are ideal for displaying the values of several items at a single point in time.

Column graphs are the best choice for displaying the variations in the value of a single item over time.

Line graphs are often used to show variations in the values of more than one item over time.

Area graphs are like line graphs except that they plot multiple data series as cumulative layers with different colors, patterns, or shades.

Pie charts are good for displaying the percentages of an item that can be assigned to the item's components.

XY (scatter) graphs are great for plotting two values to see if there is any correlation between them.

Combination graphs can show two different types of graphs at once; for example, combinations of line and bar graphs, or bar and area graphs.

3D graphs are useful for displaying data with two or more variables. 3D formats are available for the following types of graphs: line, bar, column, area, and pie.

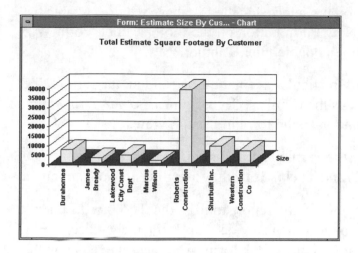

5. Choose Exit & Return To Form from the File menu to see the effects of your changes. The graph reflects the changes you made in the Graph program, but because of the size of the Detail section of the form, things look a bit cramped.

6. Maximize the Form window, and in Design view, adjust the size of the Detail section until the graph looks the way it did in Graph's Chart window.

You can make many more formatting changes in Graph, including changing the font size and style, and adding elements such as text and arrows. Feel free to experiment with the graph you have created or to create more graphs based on the data in the sample database.

Adding a Graph as a Subform

Earlier in the chapter, you learned how to use a query to combine the names in the Customers table with the estimate sizes in the Estimates table. Sometimes, however, the data you want to include from one table may be too extensive to fit on a graph. For example, suppose you want to see the customers' addresses as well as their names. You cannot easily show the addresses on the graph, but you can create a regular form and embed the graph as a subform. Follow the steps below:

1. Click the Form window's Restore button to restore its previous size, and then close the window, saving your changes.

2. With Customers selected in the Database window's table list, click the New Form button on the toolbar, click Form Wizards, and then double-click Tabular.

3. Display all the fields except the Log field on the form, select Embossed as the form's style, assign *Customer Estimates* as the title, and open the form in Design view.

4. Maximize the Form window, and tighten up the arrangement of controls and labels so that they are all visible on the screen.

5. Use the Subform/Subreport tool in the Toolbox to place a subform about 5 inches wide and 3 1/4 inches deep in the Form Footer section of the form. (If a message tells you that the form will be shown in single-form view, click OK.)

6. In the Properties window, select the Estimate Size By CustomerID form—the graph—as the Source Object, and type *CustomerID* in both the Link Child Fields and Link Master Fields edit boxes.

7. Switch to Form view to see these results:

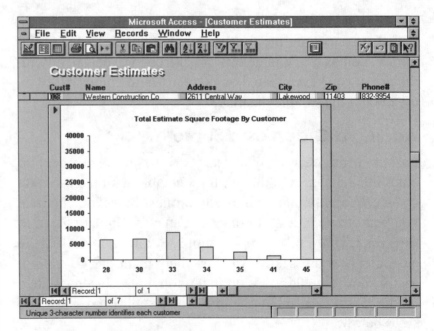

Print Preview

After you design a form, you can see how it will look if you print it by clicking the Print Preview button on the toolbar. In Print Preview, the form's text is generally too small to be legible, but you can click the Zoom button on the Print Preview toolbar to zoom in for a closer look. Click the Print button to print the form directly from Print Preview.

8. Use the scroll buttons at the bottom of the Form window to display the names and addresses of each customer. When you are ready, close the window, saving the new form as *Estimate Size By Customer (chart)*.

As an alternative, you could have opened a blank form and embedded both a tabular form with customer information and the Estimate Size By CustomerID graph. You would then have been able to see the information for all the customers at the same time.

Graphs can be useful tools for displaying information in a database. They are also fun. To begin with, it may take several attempts before you can get the graph exactly right. Microsoft Graph provides many ways of showing your data, and it's worth exploring and perfecting your graphing skills.

5
Using Reports
to Print Information

Fred Anderson
943 Spruce Circle
Lakewood, FL 11403

Jonathan Bray
5941 Hilltop Road
Lakewood, FL 11403

Lance Bright
148 Center St., #B211
Pinedale, FL 11415

Jeffrey Davis
1171 Simpson Heights
Lakewood, FL 11403

Linda Gardner
8841 Market Street
Lakewood, FL 11403

James Murray
7921 Port Avenue
Lakewood, FL 11403

Richard Talbot
1109 Emerson Way
Lakewood, FL 11403

Bid

18-Apr-94

Shurbuilt Inc.

966 8th Street

Lakewood   FL   11403

884-8742

**We submit the following bid for performing the
roofing services you requested. The total bid
price includes any extra items this job requires.
The extra items are listed for your convenience.**

Estimate number: E04-94-01

Job size in square feet: 2480

Extra items: New gutters

Cost of extra items: $590.00

Total bid: $3,716.68

Forms vs. reports

In Chapter 4, you developed ways to look at and work with data in forms, which let you view and control information from various sources. Although you can print a form, its primary function is as an interactive tool on your computer screen. The purpose of a report, on the other hand, is to extract information from a database and show it on the printed page. So when you need a neatly formatted hard copy of sorted and grouped information, consider using a report.

Creating Single-Table Reports

Creating a report is similar to creating a form. The first few steps are the same, except that you accomplish them with Report Wizards instead of Form Wizards. To start exploring reports, let's create a single-table, single-column report based on the Jobs table:

1. Close all open windows except the Database window.

Using the default report format

2. Select Jobs in the table list, and then click AutoReport on the toolbar. After a few seconds, Access displays this report:

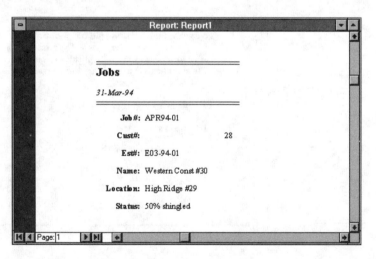

Print Preview

Because reports are usually created to produce printouts, Access displays the report in Print Preview so that you can see what it will look like on the page.

Zooming out

3. Click the Zoom button on the toolbar to zoom out for a bird's eye view:

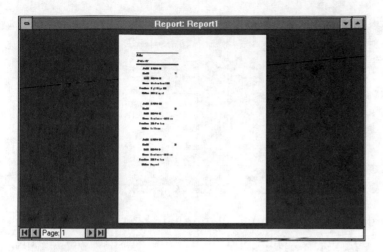

4. Click the Zoom button again to zoom back in, and then, using the scroll buttons in the bottom left corner of the screen, scroll from page to page to see how the report will be printed.

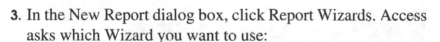 Zooming in

As you scroll, notice that the records will be printed in job order. Suppose you want to sort the records by customer instead of by job. Follow these steps:

1. Double-click the Report window's Control menu icon to close the window, and click No when Access asks whether you want to save the report.

2. With Jobs selected in the Database window's table list, click the New Report button on the toolbar.

3. In the New Report dialog box, click Report Wizards. Access asks which Wizard you want to use:

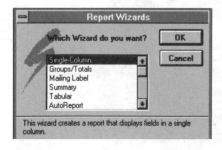

4. Click OK to accept the Single-Column option. Access then displays the first Single-Column Report Wizard dialog box shown on the next page.

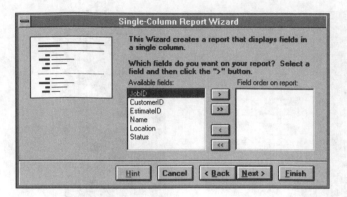

5. Click the >> button to move all the available fields to the Field Order box on the right, and then click Next to display the second dialog box:

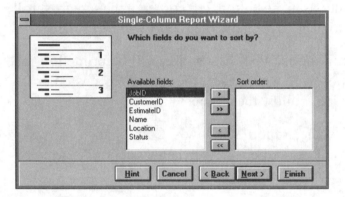

Sorting by customer

6. Double-click the CustomerID field to move it to the Sort Order box, and click Next to display the third dialog box:

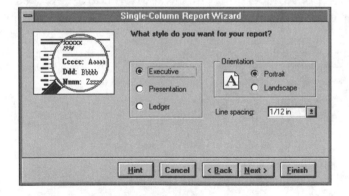

Starting from scratch

You can create a blank report by clicking the Report button in the Database window, clicking New, and then clicking Blank Report in the New Report dialog box. Access opens a new Report window containing Detail, Page Header, and Page Footer sections. You can then add controls to design the report.

7. Click Next again to accept the default Executive style for the report and display the final Single-Column Report Wizard dialog box:

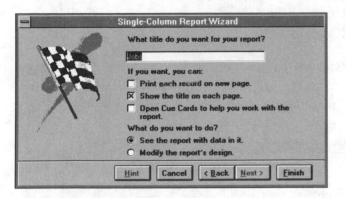

8. Click the Finish button. The new report looks the same as the previous one except that the jobs are grouped by customer.

   To make this report more useful, you could tinker with its design to reorient the information in a tabular format, with field labels in a row across the top and the corresponding field values in columns below. You could make these design changes manually, but here's an easier way:

1. Close the Report window without saving the report, and with Jobs selected in the Database window's table list, click the New Report button on the toolbar.

2. Click Report Wizards, and in the Report Wizards dialog box, select Groups/Totals, and click OK.

3. Move all the fields from the Jobs table to the Field Order box, and click Next.

4. Double-click CustomerID to move it to the Group By box, and click Next to display this dialog box:

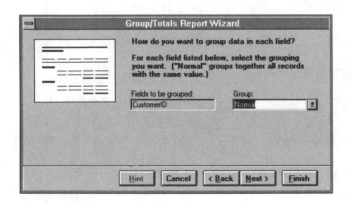

Formatting the report as a table

Summary reports

You can use the Summary Report Wizard to generate summary information from a table. For example, you can generate quarterly and/or monthly sales summaries for your customers using a summary report. Simply select the table you want to summarize, click the New Report button on the toolbar, click Report Wizards, and then double-click Summary. Access leads you through the steps necessary to create the summary report.

5. Click Next to select the default grouping. In the next dialog box, select JobID as the field to sort the groups by, and click Next.

6. Click Next again to accept Executive as the default style, change the report title to *Jobs Grouped By Customer*, and then click the Finish button. Here's the result:

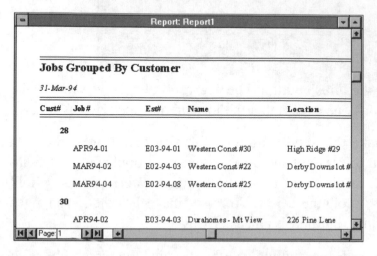

Switching to Design view

7. Click the Close Window button on the toolbar to close the Print Preview window and display the report in Design view:

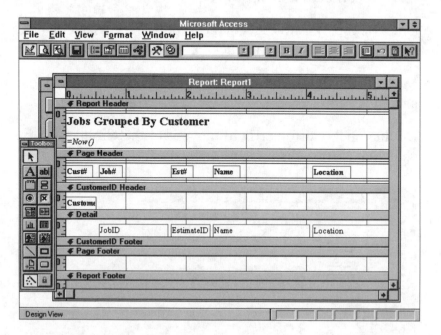

This report is a good deal more complex than the forms we looked at in Chapter 4, but the major elements are the same.

The report consists of controls placed in specific sections that determine where the control values will be printed. The report's title, Jobs Grouped By Customer, and a control that displays today's date appear in the Report Header section and will be placed once at the beginning of the report. The field names have been entered as labels in the Page Header section and will be repeated at the top of each page. Controls for the field values appear in the Detail section. Access has created a CustomerID Header section to hold the values in the CustomerID field, which you specified as the field to group the records in the Detail section by. The values in this control will be printed at the top of each group of records. All the Header sections have companion Footer sections.

Controls

Modifying the Report's Design

The Report Wizards greatly simplify the process of creating reports, but you can always modify a report's design if it doesn't quite meet your needs. Let's make a few changes to the design of this report to enhance its appearance:

1. Enlarge the CustomerID Header section by dragging the top of the Detail bar down about 1/4 inch, and then move the CustomerID control in the header down about 1/4 inch.

   Enlarging a section

2. If necessary, display the Toolbox by clicking the Toolbox button on the toolbar. Click the Line tool in the Toolbox, and draw a straight line above the CustomerID control in the CustomerID Header section, dragging the cross-hair pointer across the report until the edge of the page scrolls into view.

   Drawing lines

3. With the new line selected, open the Properties window, change the Border Width property to 2 pt, and then close the Properties window.

   Changing the width of lines

4. Click one of the lines at the bottom of the Page Header section, and press the Delete key. Repeat this step for the other line.

   Deleting lines

5. Click the Save button on the toolbar, and save the report as *Jobs Grouped By Customer*.

6. Click the Print Preview button on the toolbar to see the results shown on the next page.

   Switching to Print Preview

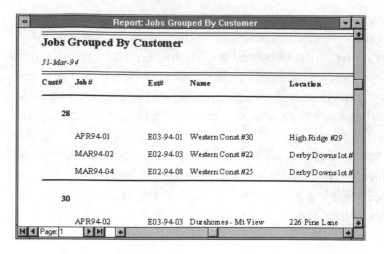

A line now separates the groups so that they are easier to distinguish.

Grouping Records

The ability to group records in reports can be very useful. For example, employees can be grouped based on their department or job title. Customers can be grouped based on their ZIP code or city. Inventory items can be grouped by location, size, cost or other criteria depending on the fields you have in the table. For this section, let's create a new report using the Materials table so that you can compare the cost per unit of similar materials. To make this comparison, you need to group the materials by type. Follow these steps:

1. Close the current Report window, and use the Report Wizards to create a new Group/Totals report based on the Materials table.

2. Select all the fields to include in the report and group the records by the ItemID field.

3. Accept Normal as the Group setting, and select the Unit-OfMeasure field to sort by.

Tabular reports

By selecting the Tabular Report Wizard, you can create a report in a simple columnar format that looks like a fancy version of the underlying database table. The data can be sorted on one or more of the table's fields, and a default Sum control displays a total for the first field.

4. Finally, select Ledger as the report style, and open this report in Print Preview:

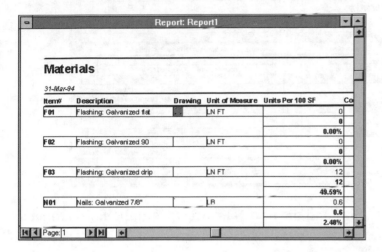

5. Save the report as *Materials*.

6. Scroll through the report, noticing any problems that need to be fixed.

You can improve the look and the function of this report in several ways. First, you can adjust the widths of the Units-Per100SF and CostPerUnit controls to show more data on the screen at one time. Second, you can adjust the grouping specification to group records by the type of item. And third, you can change the summary fields to something more appropriate for this report, since totaling the unit cost of different types of nails and shingles is not valuable in any way. Follow these steps to adjust the control widths:

1. Click the Close Window button on the toolbar to display the report in Design view.

2. Click the UnitsPer100SF control in the Page Header section, hold down the Shift key, and click each of the controls in the same column. The Report window looks like the one shown on the next page.

Adjusting the widths of several controls

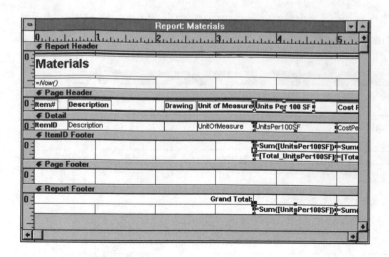

Sizing to the narrowest

3. Choose Size and then To Narrowest from the Format menu to make all the controls the same size.

4. Repeat steps 2 and 3 for the CostPerUnit set of controls, omitting the control that contains *=(Page)*, which numbers the pages of the report.

Moving several controls at once

5. With the CostPerUnit set of controls still selected, move the pointer over the controls until the pointer becomes an open hand, and then drag all the controls to the left so that they sit right next to the UnitsPer100SF controls.

6. Click the Print Preview button to see these results:

Grouping by date or time

If you select a date field to group by when designing a Group/Totals report with Report Wizards, Access gives you the option of grouping the records in your table or query by units of time from one minute up to a year. This can be useful when totaling sales for a month or quarter, or for almost any other time dependent grouping of information.

Now let's adjust the grouping specification:

1. Click the Close Window button to return to Design view.

2. Click the Sorting And Grouping button on the toolbar to display this dialog box:

Changing the grouping
specification

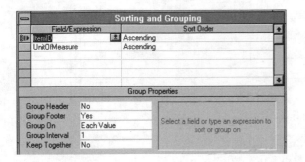

3. Because the ItemID values all begin with a letter that identifies the type of item, you can tell Access to group each type based on the first letter of the ItemID value. To do this, change the Group On option in the Group Properties section to Prefix Characters.

Grouping by prefix
characters

4. Leave the Group Interval property set to 1 to tell Access to consider only the first character of the ItemID value when grouping.

Grouping by first
character only

5. Change the Keep Together property to Whole Group so that Access will not break groups across pages, and then double-click the Control menu icon to close the dialog box.

Keeping groups on
one page

   Here's a simple way to get rid of the inappropriate summary controls:

1. In the ItemID Footer, select the Sum control in the Units-Per100SF column, and change its Visible property to No. Repeat this step for the Total control in the same column, and for both the Sum and the Total controls in the CostPerUnit column.

Hiding controls

2. Click the Report Footer bar to select it, and change its Visible property to No.

Hiding sections

3. Save all the changes you've made to the Materials report, and then click the Print Preview button on the toolbar to see the results shown on the next page.

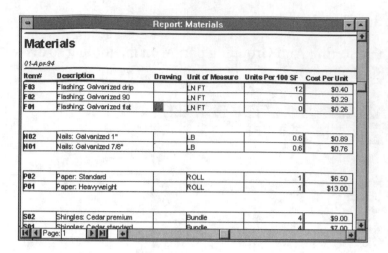

The records are now neatly grouped by the first character in the ItemID field, and the Total controls are no longer visible. This is now a useful report that can be printed and used as a basis for negotiating new materials prices with suppliers.

Summarizing Information

As you have seen, you can group records in reports in several ways. Grouping is an important means of manipulating your data's appearance in a report and is one of the major differences between reports and forms. Grouping also enables you to summarize the data by performing calculations directly in the report rather than in the underlying database table.

To demonstrate more ways of summarizing data, let's create a new Groups/Totals report for the Estimates table. Suppose you want to track the estimated cost of extra items for all roofing jobs. Specifically, you want to group estimates by month and calculate the average and total costs so that you can, for example, evaluate changes over time or compare the estimates to actual costs. Follow these steps to create the new report for the extra items:

1. Use the Estimates table and the Report Wizards to create a Groups/Totals report that displays controls for the EstimateID, CustomerID, Extras, and CostExtras fields grouped by EstimateID with the Group option set to 1st 5 Characters. Sort within groups by CustomerID, use the Ledger style, and give the report the title *Summary Of Cost Of Extra Items*. Deselect the Calculate Percentages of the Total option, and open the report in Print Preview. It looks like this:

Report: Report1

Summary of Cost of Extra Items

21-Apr-94

Est#	Cust#	Extras	Extras Cost
E02-94-01	33	Redo damaged trim	$640.00
E02-94-02	45	New trim	$800.00
E02-94-03	28	None	$0.00
E02-94-04	35	None	$0.00
E02-94-05	30	None	$0.00
E02-94-06	33	None	$0.00
E02-94-07	41	Chimney cap	$120.00
E02-94-08	28	None	$0.00
E02-94-09	33	None	$0.00
E02-94-10	45	New trim	$800.00
	351		$2,360.00
E03-94-01	28	None	$0.00
E03-94-02	45	New gutters	$710.00
E03-94-03	30	None	$0.00
E03-94-04	30	None	$0.00

Page: 1

2. Save the report as *Extras Summary*.

Access has added summary fields for the fields with the number data type. However, instead of totaling the values in the CustomerID field, you want Access to count the number of customers in each group. Follow these steps:

1. Click the Close Window button to move to Design view.

2. Click the Label tool in the Toolbox, create a label to the left of the first Sum formula in the EstimateID Footer section, and type *Number:* as the label.

3. Click the control containing the first Sum formula, and in the Properties window, change *Sum* in the Control Source edit box to *Count*. Repeat this step for the Sum formula below Grand Total in the Report Footer section.

Changing formulas

The remaining Sum formula in the EstimateID Footer section is fine, but how about adding a control that averages the costs for each month? Here's how:

1. Point to the top of the Page Footer bar, and drag it down about 1/2 inch to create space for a new control.

2. Use the Text Box tool in the Toolbox to add an unbound control below the Sum control.

Adding calculated controls

3. With the control selected, open its Properties window, click the Control Source edit box, and then click the Build button. In the Expression Builder dialog box, type =, double-click

Functions, double-click Built-In Functions, and then double-click Avg in the right box. Click *expr* in the formula—this is a placeholder (meaning *expression*) for the field whose values you want to average. Then click Extras Summary in the left box, click Field List in the middle box, and click the Paste button to replace *expr* with the highlighted field (CostExtras) in the right box. The dialog box looks like this:

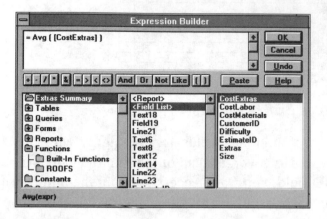

4. Click OK to transfer the formula to the Properties window.

5. Change the Format property to Currency, change the Font Weight property to Bold, and close the Properties window.

6. Select all the controls in the Extras Cost column, choose Size and then To Narrowest from the Format menu, and then move the controls to the right edge of the page.

7. Finally, use the Label tool in the Toolbox to create a *Total*: label to the left of the Sum formula and an *Average*: label to the left of the Avg formula. The report now looks like this:

Moving controls to other sections

You can drag a control and its label anywhere on a report, including from one section to another. You can't drag just a control or just a label to another section. If you need to move just a control to another section, drag the control and its label and then delete the label. However, you can't use this method to move just a label to another section; instead, use the Label tool in the Toolbox to create the label from scratch.

8. Click the Print Preview button on the toolbar to see how the report will look when printed:

	Report: Extras Summary	

Summary of Cost of Extra Items

21-Apr-94

Est#	Cust#	Extras		Extras Cost
E02-94-01	33	Redo dam aged trim		$640.00
E02-94-02	45	New trim		$800.00
E02-94-03	28	None		$0.00
E02-94-04	35	None		$0.00
E02-94-05	30	None		$0.00
E02-94-06	33	None		$0.00
E02-94-07	41	Chimney cap		$120.00
E02-94-08	28	None		$0.00
E02-94-09	33	None		$0.00
E02-94-10	45	New trim		$800.00
Number:	10		Total:	$2,360.00
			Average:	$236.00
E03-94-01	28	None		$0.00
E03-94-02	45	New gutters		$710.00

Page: 1

As you can see, the estimates are grouped by month because the Group option is set to 1st 5 Characters. The total and average amounts reflect how extra items fit into the roofing company's business. A grand total, which totals the cost of all the extra items, appears at the bottom of the report.

Setting Page Breaks

Sometimes you might want each group of information to be printed on its own page instead of as a continuous stream of data. In Access, you can set horizontal page breaks to suit your needs, but because reports are geared toward paper output, vertical page breaks are determined by the page size and orientation. (You can change these and other page characteristics in the Print Setup dialog box, which you access by clicking the Print Setup button on the Print Preview toolbar— see page 148.)

Suppose you want to print each month's information in the Extras Summary report on a separate page. To accomplish this, you need to insert a page break after the summary fields in the EstimateID Footer section. Follow these steps:

1. Switch to Design view, and click the Page Break tool in the Toolbox.

2. Move the pointer into the EstimateID Footer section, just below the Average label, and click. Access inserts a page break symbol at the left side of the section.

3. Click the Print Preview button, and then click the scroll buttons at the bottom of the window to see the results. If you click the Print button on the toolbar now, Access will produce four separate pages, one for each month.

4. Close the Extras Summary report, saving your changes.

Creating Multi-Table Reports

Just as you will often need to display information from more than one table in a form, you will often need to print information from more than one table in a report. As with forms, you combine table information by creating a subreport and embedding it in a main report.

Suppose the roofing company needs to prepare bids for jobs using the costs for labor, materials, and extra items stored in the Estimates table. The bid also needs to include customer information from the Customers table. As an example, let's prepare a bid for estimate E04-94-01. The first step is to create a subreport with the customer information:

Creating a subreport

1. Use the Report Wizards to create a new single-column report based on the Customers table. Use the Name, Address, City, PostalCode, and Phone fields, sort by the Name field, accept the default Executive style and the default title, and open the report in Design view.

Removing sections

2. Choose Page Header/Footer from the Format menu, and click OK to delete its controls. Repeat this step with the Report Header/Footer command.

3. Delete all the labels (not the controls) in the Detail section.

4. Use the Label tool in the Toolbox to create a label to the right of the City control. Type *FL* as the label, and then change its Font Weight property to Normal and its Text Align property to Left.

5. Arrange the PostalCode and Phone controls as shown here:

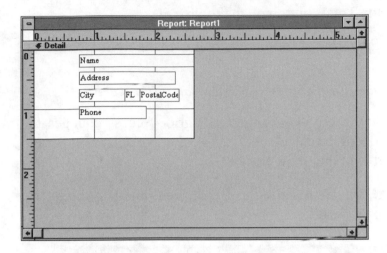

6. Reduce the size of the report (the white area) by dragging the bottom border up below the Phone control.

Reducing the report's size

7. Click the Print Preview button, and scroll the records to make sure everything looks OK.

8. Finally, close the Report window, saving the report as *Bid Customers*.

You have completed the first phase of bid preparation. Later, you will embed this report as a subreport of the final product. But first you need to create the main report.

Just as you can use a query as the information source for a form, you can use a query as the source for a main report or a subreport. In this case, the query will extract fields from the Estimates table, calculate a total bid that allows a 20 percent margin on materials and labor, and extract the record needed for the E04-94-01 bid report. Follow these steps:

Basing reports on queries

1. With Estimates selected in the Database window's table list, click the New Query button on the toolbar, and then click the New Query button.

2. Add the EstimateID, CustomerID, Size, Extras, and Cost-Extras fields to the QBE grid, and adjust the width of the columns so that you can see all the fields.

3. Next, type *E04-94-01* in the Criteria row of the EstimateID column.

4. Click the Totals button on the toolbar.

5. In the Field row of the empty column to the right of the Cost-Extras field, type

Total: Sum([CostExtras]+([CostMaterials]+[CostLabor])*1.2)

6. Click anywhere else in the QBE grid. Access changes the Total row of the calculated field's column to Grouped By and puts an X in the Show box.

7. Change the Total setting to Expression, and run the query. Here is the result:

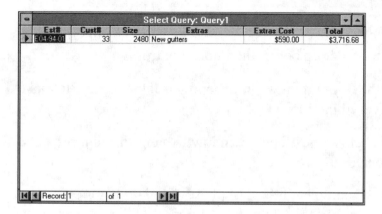

The query datasheet shows one record for estimate E04-94-01 with the bid total in the last field.

8. Close the Select Query window, saving the query as *Bid Information*.

You now have the two elements you need for the bid report. Follow these steps to create the main report and embed the Bid Customers subreport in it:

1. Use the Report Wizards to create a new single-column report based on the Bid Information query. Use the EstimateID, Size, Extras, CostExtras, and Total fields, sort on the EstimateID field, select the Executive style, type *Bid* as the title, and open the report in Design view.

2. Save the report as *Bid Report*.

3. Enlarge the Detail section to about 5 inches by 5 inches. (Move the pointer to the bottom right corner, and when the

Sizing the active area

In Design view, the Detail section of the report can be made wider or narrower by dragging the border on the right side of the white active area. If you double-click in the gray area to the right of the active area, Access opens the Properties window for the entire report.

pointer changes to a four-headed arrow, drag down and to the right, using the rulers to gauge how far to drag.)

4. Select all the controls and their labels, and drag them down and to the right until the EstimateID control sits 3 inches from the top and 2 inches from the left side of the Detail section.

5. Adjust the sizes and positions of the controls and labels, and change the labels as shown here:

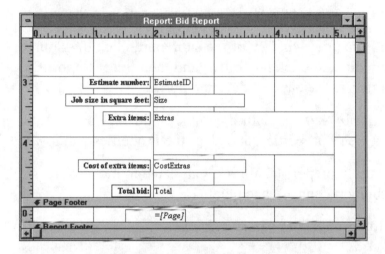

6. Change the Text Align property of all the controls to Left.

7. Click the Line tool in the Toolbox, and draw a line all the way across the page between the CostExtras and Total controls. Change the line's Border Width property to 2 pt.

8. Now scroll up, add a label, and type the text shown here:

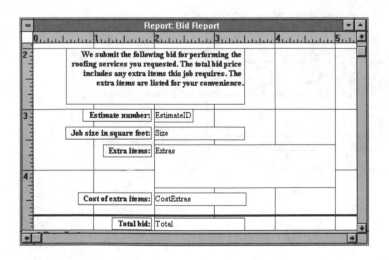

Adjusting lines

If you have difficulty drawing a straight line, use the Properties window to fix the problem. The Height property indicates how far up or down a line slopes from its point of origin, not its length. To make the line straight, change the Height property to 0. To specify the exact length of a line, use the Width property. (Other types of controls also have Height and Width properties you can use to help with the precise placement or sizing of controls.)

9. Click outside the label, and then click the label to select its box. Next, click the Left-Align Text button on the toolbar to left-align the label's text.

You have summarized the bid information from the Estimates table in the report. Now you need to merge the customer information from the Bid Customers report as a subreport. Follow these steps:

Merging the main report and subreport

1. Click the Subform/Subreport tool in the Toolbox, and create a subreport control at the top of the Detail section of the report.

2. In the Properties window of the subreport, click the Source Object edit box, click the arrow, and then select Report.Bid Customers as the basis of the subreport.

3. Type *CustomerID* as both the Link Child Fields and Link Master Fields properties, and close the Properties window.

4. Select the subreport label (you may have to move or resize the subreport control), and delete it.

Now for a couple of cosmetic changes:

1. Select one of the lines above *Bid* in the Page Header section, extend the line across the page, and set its Border Width property to 2 pt.

Properties shortcut

When you need to change the same property for several adjacent objects on a report or form, you can either Shift-click to select all the objects, or you can drag an imaginary box around the objects. To drag a box, point to where you want the top left corner of the box to be, then hold down the left mouse button, and drag to the bottom right corner of the box, making sure that the box covers all the objects you want to include in the selection. When you release the mouse button, Access selects all the objects inside the imaginary box. You can then display a common Properties window for the objects.

2. Select and delete the second line above *Bid*. (It's probably sitting on top of the Bid control's border.)

3. Repeat steps 1 and 2 for the lines below *=Now()* in the Page Header section. Here are the results:

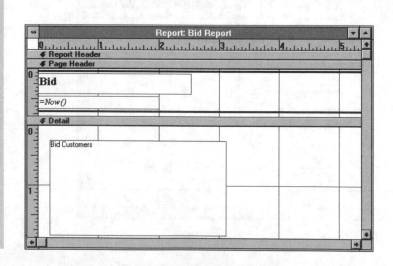

4. Scroll down, and select and delete =*[Page]* in the Page Footer section.

5. Look at the report in Print Preview. If necessary, resize or re-align the controls to achieve a balanced, good-looking report.

6. When you are finished, close and save the report.

This process has been a little long, but you now have a report that can be used to produce a bid for any estimate. Whenever you complete the work on an estimate, you can change the criteria in the Bid Information query to reflect the new estimate number, open the Bid Report report, and print it. (See page 148 for information about printing.) When you print the report, Access executes the query, pulls the information from the query datasheet into the main report, and pulls the correct customer information from the Customers table through the subreport. Pretty impressive stuff! So it's worthwhile taking the time to set up reports to perform routine tasks whenever possible.

Reusing the Bid Report

Creating Mailing Labels

We'll take just a quick detour to demonstrate another Access Report Wizard: Mailing Labels. Once you learn how to use the wizard, you'll wish all programs made creating mailing labels this easy.

Suppose the roofing company occasionally sends out information to its employees about benefits. To save time, you want to create a mailing label report that can be used to print a set of current labels whenever they are needed. Follow the steps below:

1. Close any open windows except the Database window, select Employees in the Database window's table list, and click the New Report button on the toolbar. Then click Report Wizards, and double-click Mailing Label. Access displays the first Mailing Label Wizard dialog box, as shown on the following page.

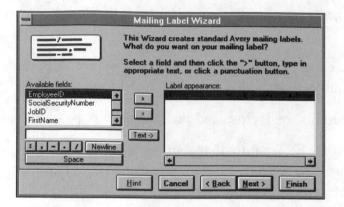

The fields are listed for inclusion on the label as usual, but this dialog box also displays several buttons that resemble keyboard keys, including a Space (Spacebar) button, a Newline (Enter) button, several punctuation buttons, and a Text button. You use these buttons to specify how the label should be laid out.

Entering fields in the label

2. Double-click the FirstName field to add it to the first line in the Label Appearance box, and then click the Space button to insert a space.

3. Double-click the LastName field to add it after the space, and then click the Newline button to create a second line.

4. Double-click the Address field, and click the Newline button to create a third line.

5. Double-click the City field, click the Comma button, and click the Space button. Then click the edit box to the left of the Text button, type *FL*, and click the Text button to add FL to the third line of the label. Finally, click the Space button twice, and double-click the PostalCode field to finish the third line.

Specifying a sort field

6. Click Next, specify LastName as the sort field, and click Next again to display a dialog box in which Access asks you to specify a label format. (You can select the format by Avery number or by the size and number of labels in a row. The list of available formats varies, depending on your printer's capabilities.)

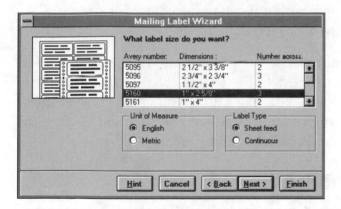

7. Select the size you want (we selected Avery 5160), and click
Next to display this dialog box:

Specifying the label format

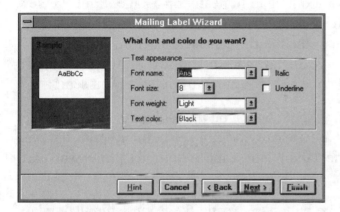

8. Change the font size to 10 and the font weight to Bold, and
click Next. Then click Finish to see the labels in Print Preview
(your screen will reflect the label format you selected):

Setting the font and size

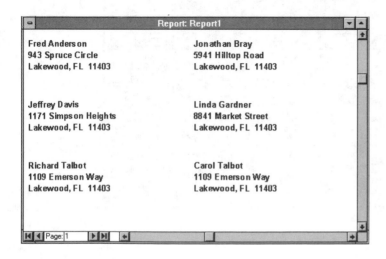

9. Save the report with a meaningful name; for example, we saved our report as *5160 Labels*.

As with other reports, you can also use queries as the information source for labels. For example, to send information to customers in a specific sales area, you could create a query that extracts information by city or ZIP code and then use the query as the basis for the mailing labels.

Printing Reports

You have looked at reports in Print Preview several times to get an idea of how they will look when printed. Using Print Preview can save you a lot of time and paper. If your report is too wide or too long to fit neatly on a page, Print Preview shows the overflow pages and allows you to change the report's design or modify the print setup before you commit it to paper. We've already shown you several ways to change the design; here we'll look at modifying the print setup:

Setting print options

1. Click the Print Setup button on the toolbar to open the Print Setup dialog box where you can select many print options, including orientation (landscape or portrait), printer and port, and margins.

2. Click the More button to expand the Print Setup dialog box to include other options related to size, layout, and spacing:

Printing properties

One property you can set for an entire report is the Fast Laser Printing property. Setting this property to Yes (the default) speeds up printing on most newer laser printers by replacing lines and rectangles with rules. Another print-related property is Layout For Print. If the fonts on your printed reports don't match those on your screen, check that this property is set to Yes so that what you see on the screen matches what you see in print.

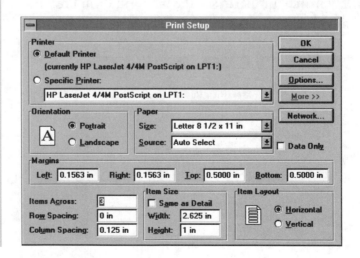

3. All the options have been set to print the mailing labels you created in the previous section, so click Cancel to close the dialog box without changing anything.

Now let's give the printer some work to do:

1. Click the Print button on the toolbar to display this dialog box:

Printing the report

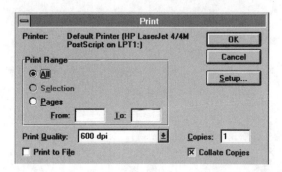

Here you can specify the number of copies to print, which pages of the report to print, and the print quality setting in dots per inch. You can also open the Print Setup dialog box from here.

More print options

2. When you are satisfied with all the settings in the Print dialog box, click OK to print the report displayed in the Print Preview window.

In this chapter, we have given you only a glimpse of the potential of Access reports, in the expectation that you will learn more about them as you use them. If you want more practice, our sample reports give you many ways to experiment with manipulating various fields of data in printed presentations. Remember, this experimentation has no effect on the structure of the underlying database tables or the data they contain.

Automating Routine Tasks

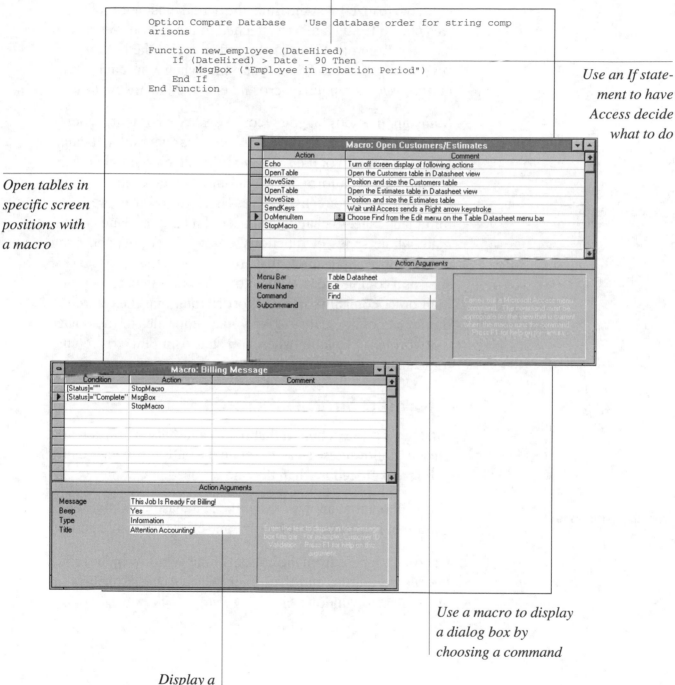

*Display a warning
message with a five-
line module*

```
Option Compare Database    'Use database order for string comp
arisons

Function new_employee (DateHired)
    If (DateHired) > Date - 90 Then
        MsgBox ("Employee in Probation Period")
    End If
End Function
```

*Use an If state-
ment to have
Access decide
what to do*

*Open tables in
specific screen
positions with
a macro*

Macro: Open Customers/Estimates

Action	Comment
Echo	Turn off screen display of following actions
OpenTable	Open the Customers table in Datasheet view
MoveSize	Position and size the Customers table
OpenTable	Open the Estimates table in Datasheet view
MoveSize	Position and size the Estimates table
SendKeys	Wait until Access sends a Right arrow keystroke
DoMenuItem	Choose Find from the Edit menu on the Table Datasheet menu bar
StopMacro	

Action Arguments

Menu Bar	Table Datasheet
Menu Name	Edit
Command	Find
Subcommand	

Macro: Billing Message

Condition	Action	Comment
[Status]=""	StopMacro	
[Status]="Complete"	MsgBox	
	StopMacro	

Action Arguments

Message	This Job Is Ready For Billing!
Beep	Yes
Type	Information
Title	Attention Accounting!

*Use a macro to display
a dialog box by
choosing a command*

*Display a
reminder with
a simple macro*

You have now seen how to use Access for Windows to create a relational database from which you can extract the information needed for daily tasks and decision-making. In Chapter 4, we showed you how to create a button that you can click to close a form. Although you may not have realized it at the time, the actual closing of the form was controlled by a macro attached to the button. When you used the Command Button Wizard to create the button, Access set up this macro for you, and when you clicked the button, Access ran the macro and executed its instructions.

Many applications let you record keystrokes or write macros to automate routine tasks. Access goes far beyond that capability. At one end of the scale, you can attach a simple macro to an object on a form, as we did in Chapter 4. At the other end of the scale, you can use Access Basic, a powerful programming language, to change menus and their commands, automate whole series of functions, customize forms, and even design entire applications that are dedicated to specific tasks, such as a complete order/inventory/accounting package for a mail order company. In this short chapter, we'll explore the lighter end of the scale to give you a better idea of the power that becomes available when you start using macros to customize Access databases.

Access Basic

Creating Simple Macros

First, let's create a button that opens another form when you click it. Follow these steps to set up the button's macro, using a different procedure than the one we used in Chapter 4:

A macro that opens a form

1. Close all open windows except the Database window, select Customer Log in the list of forms, and click the Design button.

2. Choose Database from the bottom of the Window menu, click the Macro button, and then click New. Access displays an empty Macro window:

In Design view, the Macro window resembles a Table window. The macro's actions and comments describing the actions appear in the top part of the window, and additional information needed to carry out the action appears in the bottom part.

The Macro window

3. Move the Macro window to the right so that you can see both its Action column and the Database window at the same time.

4. Click Employee Job Assignments in the Database window's form list, and drag it to the first Action line in the Macro window. Access inserts OpenForm in the column and Employee Job Assignments in the Form Name edit box, as shown here:

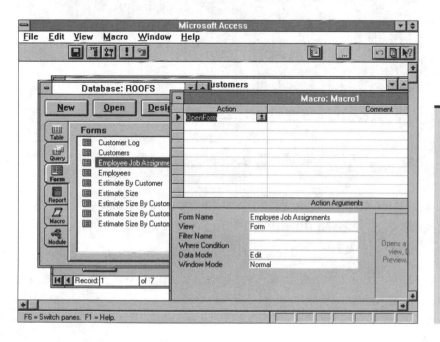

The OpenForm action arguments

In addition to entering the form's name in the Form Name edit box, Access sets the View property to Form, the Data Mode to Edit, and the Window Mode to Normal. If you want, you can change these properties to determine how the form is displayed when you run the macro.

5. Press Tab to move to the Comment column, and type *Opens the Employee Job Assignments form in Form view*.

6. Close the Macro window, saving the macro as *Open Job Assignments*.

Now let's assign the new macro to a button on the Customer Log form:

Assigning the macro to a button

1. Activate Customer Log's Form window, which should be in Design view, and position the window so that you can just see the Close button when the Database window is active.

2. Drag Open Job Assignments from the Database window's macro list to the blank area to the right of the Customer Log's Close button. When you release the mouse button, Access creates a new command button.

3. Resize the button so that its label is visible, like this:

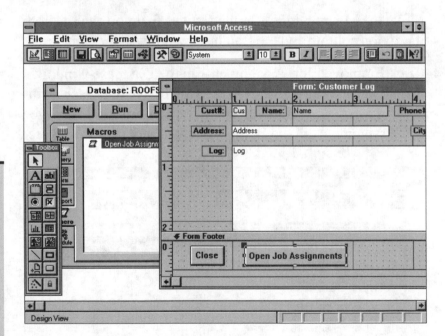

Macro comments

Although entering comments in the Comment column of the Macro window may seem like a waste of time, it can save your bacon down the road when you return to modify or debug a macro. Comments can help you decipher the somewhat cryptic instructions in each line of a macro so that you know exactly what the macro does. We highly recommend including comments in all your macros.

4. Switch to Form view, and test the new macro by clicking the Open Job Assignments button. Access obediently opens the specified form.

5. Close both open forms, saving the changes to Customer Log.

Opening Two Tables at Once

Suppose you often find yourself looking at both the Estimates and Customers tables. You could create a form showing the information in both tables, but you would rather look at the tables themselves. Follow these steps to open both tables with a couple of clicks of the mouse:

1. Click New in the Database window to create a new macro.

2. Click the arrow to display a list of available actions, scroll the list, and select OpenTable.

3. Click the Table Name edit box in the Action Arguments section, click the arrow, and select Customers from the list of available tables.

4. Click the Comment line, type an appropriate description, and press Tab to move to the next line. (From now on, we won't tell you what comments to include.)

5. Click the arrow, and select MoveSize from the list of actions. Then type *0* as the Right and Down arguments, *8* as the Width argument, and *2* as the Height argument. (These arguments refer to the position and size in inches of the table in the Access workspace.)

6. In the third Action line, select OpenTable, and select Estimates as the Table Name argument.

7. In the fourth Action line, select MoveSize, and set the arguments as follows: Right *0*, Down *2*, Width *8*, and Height *3*.

8. Close the Macro window, saving the macro as *Open Customers/Estimates*.

Now let's run the macro:

1. Select the Open Customers/Estimates macro in the Database window, and click the Run button. The result is shown on the next page.

A macro that opens tables

If MoveSize doesn't work

If you try using the MoveSize action in a macro to size and position a window and it doesn't work, check the size of the window that was active before you ran the macro. If the active window is maximized, any new windows the macro opens will also be maximized. Simply reduce the size of the active window, and run the macro again.

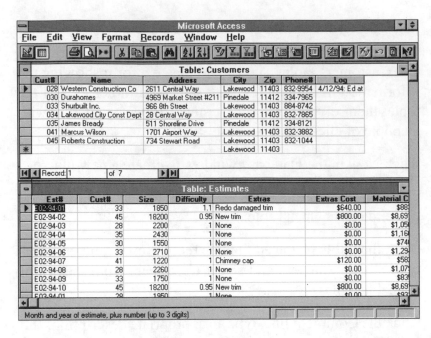

Both tables are displayed in the positions specified in the Action Arguments section of the macro. Using this macro saves time because you no longer have to open and resize each table individually every time you need to see both tables.

Modifying Macros

After you use a macro for a while, you'll usually find ways to improve it. For example, suppose you frequently search the Estimates table for records for a particular customer number. You want to add a couple of actions to those performed by the Open Customers/Estimates macro so that Access goes to the CustomerID field in the Estimates table and opens the Find dialog box. Follow these steps to add the necessary actions:

SendKeys caution

Be very careful when you use the Up Arrow, Down Arrow, Left Arrow, or Right Arrow key designations as the Keystrokes argument for the SendKeys action. If you subsequently change the design of the table, form, query, or report you use with the macro, you could end up in a different field or record than you intended.

1. Close the Estimates and Customers tables, and open the Open Customers/Estimates macro in Design view.

2. Click the fifth Action line, select the SendKeys action, type *{Right}* as the Keystrokes argument, and change the Wait argument to Yes. This instruction tells Access to move to the right one field before processing the next instruction.

3. In the sixth Action line, select the DoMenuItem action, set the Menu Bar argument to Table Datasheet, leave the Menu

Name argument set to Edit, and set the Command argument to Find. Working from bottom to top, you are telling Access to choose the Find command from the Edit menu of the Table Datasheet menu bar.

4. In the seventh Action line, select the StopMacro action.

5. Close the Macro window, saving the changes.

6. Now run the macro to see the results.

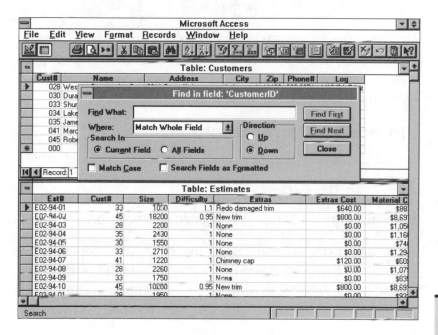

As the macro runs, you can see Access step through the macro's instructions, opening the tables, moving to the right one field, and then opening the Find dialog box. Access accomplishes these tasks pretty quickly, but processing a complex macro can be slow when the computer has to continually update the image on the screen. You can speed things up by showing only the results of a macro, not the intermediate steps. Here's how to show only the results of the Open Customers/ Estimates macro:

1. Close the Find dialog box and the Estimates and Customers tables, and open the Open Customers/Estimates macro in Design view.

Stepping through macros

The toolbar displayed when you are designing a macro includes a Single Step button. When you click this button, Access displays a dialog box you can use to walk through the current macro one step at a time. Use the other options in the dialog box to halt or continue the step-through process. Stepping through a macro is a convenient way to zero in on any errors that might be present. When you're finished, click the Single Step button again to return to normal processing.

2. Click the first row selector to select the entire line, press the Insert key to add a blank line at the top of the macro, click the new blank Action line, and select Echo.

3. Change the Echo On argument to No and type *MACRO RUNNING* in the Status Bar Text edit box.

4. Close the Macro window, saving the changes.

5. Now run the macro, watching for the message in the status bar at the bottom of the screen.

Because this macro and the processing time are short, the message appears for only a moment. However, if you were running a macro that included queries on large tables, not showing the screen updates could save time.

Macros That Make Decisions

Sometimes you will need a macro to process part or all of it's actions only if certain conditions prevail at the time. For example, you could attach a macro to a report so that the report is printed only if the report is opened between specific dates.

As a demonstration, we'll use a macro to flag a job as ready for billing whenever the value in the Status field of the job's record in the Jobs table is changed to Complete. This macro will ensure that invoices are sent out promptly. First let's create a basic form for data entry:

1. Close any windows you may have open except the Database window, select Jobs in the table list, click the New Form button, and use the Form Wizards to create a standard, single-column form that uses all the fields in the table. Assign the title *Job Add/Update*, and open the form in Form view.

2. Close the Form window, saving the form as *Job Add/Update*.

Next, you need to attach a conditional macro to the form. Here are the steps:

1. In the Database window, click the Macro button, and then click the New button to display a blank Macro window. Click the Save button, and save the macro as *Billing Message*.

Blank lines

Feel free to add a blank line wherever needed in a macro so that you can put a comment in the Comment column but leave both the Action and Comment columns empty. That way, you can add an explanation about the purpose of the macro or include a note to yourself without interfering with the macro's processing.

2. Click the Conditions button on the toolbar to add a Condition column to the top section of the Macro window, and type *[Status]= " "* in the first Condition line. Click the first Action line, and select StopMacro from the list. The first line tells Access to stop running the macro if the Status field is empty (" " essentially means *nothing*).

3. Click the second Condition line, type *[Status]= "Complete"*, and in the second Action line, select MsgBox as the action. Then type *This Job Is Ready For Billing!* as the Message argument and *Attention Accounting!* as the Title argument. Leave the Beep argument set to Yes, but change the Type argument to Information. The second line tells Access to display an information style message box with the specified title and message.

4. Skip over the third Condition line, and in the third Action line, select StopMacro. With the second line selected, the macro looks like this:

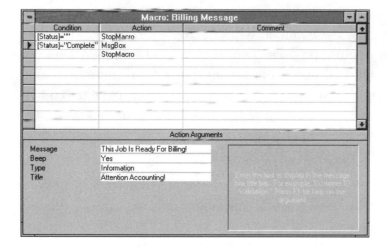

5. Close the Macro window, saving the changes when prompted.

You are now ready to attach the macro to the Job Add/Update form. Follow these steps:

1. Open the Job Add/Update form in Design view, and then open the form's Properties window.

A sequence of conditional actions

If you want Access to perform a sequence of actions when a single condition is met, put the actions one after the other in the Action column and precede all the actions after the first with ... in the Condition column. Each ellipsis tells Access that the action on that line is part of the response to the condition established earlier. All the actions for the condition must be in consecutive rows.

2. Scroll down the properties list until you see the On Current property. Click its edit box, click the arrow, and select Billing Message from the list of available macros.

3. Close the Properties window, and save the changes to the form.

4. Switch to Form view, and scroll through the records one by one. When you reach the sixth record, a message box with the title and message you specified in the macro opens like this:

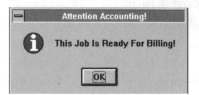

The big *i* in the blue circle indicates this meassage is for your information only. Each time you display a record that is complete, Access will display this message box.

Macros are great tools for automating the functions you perform on a regular basis. We have touched on only a few of the things you can do with macros—just enough to allow you to explore on your own. If you want to experiment but are concerned about corrupting your data, remember that you can always copy a table or even an entire database so that you can be creative while protecting your original data.

Working with Modules

You have seen that macros are simple lines of instructions that can be used to automate many common tasks, such as opening tables and finding records. Access also offers a second tool for streamlining your work with databases: *modules*. Modules are chunks of programming code written in the Access Basic programming language. They can be short and simple, or long and complex. In both cases, they can expand the power

Storing related macros in one Macro window

You can store related macros in one Macro window by making them all part of a macro group. To create the group, click the Macro Names button on the toolbar to insert a Macro Name column in the Macro window. Then enter a name in this column to the left of the first instruction of each individual macro. When you save the macro, the name you enter is assigned to the entire group. To run one of the macros in the group, choose Run Macro from the File menu, select the macro from the drop-down list, or type the name assigned to the group, a period, and the name you typed in the Macro Name column, and then click OK.

of Access beyond the interactive functions and commands we have used up to this point. In this section, we give you a brief glimpse of modules.

If you are familiar with other Microsoft Basic programming languages, then you already understand how modules work. Each module consists of units of code called *procedures*. A simple module might contain just one simple procedure. A more complex module might contain many procedures. Procedures come in different flavors; for example, some respond to specific events, and some perform specific calculations, or functions. We stick with function procedures for our examples.

Procedures

In Chapter 3, we created a query that calculated the material and labor costs for the estimates in the Estimates table. You may remember that the labor cost formula was similar to the material cost formula with the addition of a job difficulty factor and a profit factor. As a simple demonstration of a function procedure, let's create a module that simplifies the formula for the labor cost by basing it on the material cost. We can then use the module in any form or report that needs the cost information, instead of having to build the formula from scratch each time. Follow these steps to create the form you will use with the module:

1. Close any open windows except the Database window, and create a standard, single-column form based on the Estimates table. Use all the fields, assign the title *Estimate Update*, and open the form in Form view.

2. Close the form, saving it as *Estimate Update*.

Now let's create the module that will be attached to the form:

1. Click the Module button in the Database window, and then click the New button. Access opens a Module window like the one shown on the next page with a standard Option Compare Database opening line.

Creating a module

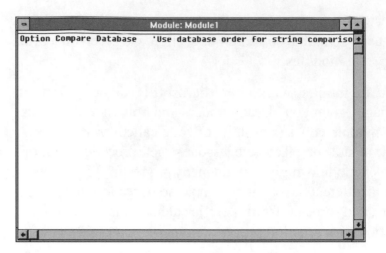

Entering a function
procedure

2. Without moving the blinking insertion point on the second line, type

Function labor_cost (material, difficulty)

and press Enter. The Option Compare Database line disappears, and Access adds an End Function line below the new blank line. You type all the instructions for this function between the Function and End Function lines.

3. Press Tab to indent the first instruction, and type

*labor_cost = (material) * (difficulty) * 1.2*

The module now looks like this:

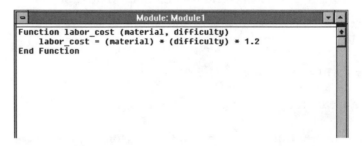

Arguments

You have just written a function procedure called *labor_cost* that uses two items of information—*material* and *difficulty*—called *arguments*. These arguments are placeholders for the values that will be used when you attach the module to a form or report. The actual work of the module will be carried out by the middle line—the formula for calculating the labor cost. This formula includes the two arguments and the constant 1.2, which is the profit factor.

4. Without pressing Enter, choose Compile Loaded Modules from the Run menu. If you made any mistakes when typing the function—for example, if you left out a required parenthesis—Access displays an error message and moves the insertion point to the line containing the error. Correct the mistake, and choose Compile Loaded Modules again.

Checking for errors

5. Close the module, saving it as *Labor Cost*.

You can now attach the module to the Estimate Update form:

1. Open the form in Design view, and if necessary, enlarge the Form window so that you can see all the controls in the Detail section.

Attaching a module to a form

2. Click the CostLabor control (not its label), display its Properties window, click the Control Source edit box, and type

=labor_cost([CostMaterials],[Difficulty])

You have told Access that the value of the CostLabor control is the result of the labor_cost function procedure calculated with the values in the CostMaterials field as the first argument and the values in the Difficulty field as the second argument.

3. Close the Properties window, save the changes to the form, and switch to Form view.

Now let's test the function:

1. Add a new record to the Estimates table via the Estimate Update form, using an estimate number of *E04-94-02*, a customer number of *33*, a size of *2480*, a difficulty of *1.1*, and a material cost of *$1,200*. Access calculates the labor cost as shown here:

Testing the function procedure

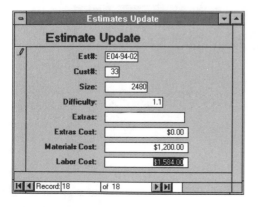

2. Close the form, saving the changes.

As you can see, using modules can simplify your work in Access. If you can keep your functions generic enough, you can use them wherever they are needed, simply by specifying the appropriate arguments each time in the Properties window of the affected control.

Modules That Make Decisions

Using an If statement ———→

Like macros, modules can also be set up to operate when specific conditions are met. One type of conditional function procedure uses an If statement to look at a value and perform one or more operations depending on what it finds. For example, suppose all the roofing company's new employee's serve a probationary period for their first 90 days and you want to know which employees are still in this probationary period when assigning employees to jobs. Follow these steps to create a module that displays a message if an employee has been on the job for less than 90 days.

1. In the Database window, click the Module button, and then click New.

2. Type *Function new_employee (DateHired)*, and press Enter.

3. Press Tab, type *If (DateHired) > Date - 90 Then* and then press Enter.

4. On the next line, press Tab, type *MsgBox ("Employee in Probation Period")*, and press Enter.

5. On the next line, type *End If* to complete the conditional procedure, which looks like this:

Formatting for readability

Using the Tab key to indent lines of code does not affect the procedure's action, but it does affect the readability of your modules. Liberal, and consistent, use of the Tab key makes it easy to see where sections of procedures begin and end.

```
Module: New Employee
Function new_employee (DateHired)
    If (DateHired) > Date - 90 Then
        MsgBox ("Employee in Probation Period")
    End If
End Function
```

You have told Access to look at the hire date of an employee and display a message if the date is within the past 90 days.

6. Access evaluates cach line of code as you enter it, so if you make a mistake typing any part of the procedure, Access may display an error message. For good measure, choose Compile Loaded Modules from the Run menu to check your work.

7. If all is well, close the Module window, saving the module as *New Employee*.

Now let's attach the module to the Employee Job Assignments form you created in Chapter 4. You may recall that the cmployee portion of this form is a subform called Employees. To attach the new_employee function procedure to the Employees subform, follow these steps:

1. Open the Employees form in Design view, click the EmployeeID control (only *Emp* is visible), and open its Properties window.

2. Scroll down, type *=new_employee([DateHired])* with no spaces in the On Enter edit box, and close the Properties window.

3. Close the Employees form, saving the changes.

You have told Access that when you move to a new record in the Employees table, it is to run the new_employee procedure using the value in the DateHired field as its argument. As you can see, part of using procedures efficiently is putting them in the right place. Specifying that the procedure should be run On Exit or After Update would not have produced the results you want.

Now let's test the procedure:

1. Open the Employees table in Datasheet view, and change Jeffrey Davis's hire date so that it is within 90 days of to-day's date.

2. Close the Table window, and open the Employee Job Assignment form.

Importing modules from other databases

If you write a module for one database and want to use it in another, you can import the module using the Import command on the File menu. In the Data Source dialog box, click Microsoft Access, and then click OK to display the Select Microsoft Access Database dialog box. Then select the database file you want, and click OK. Finally, select Module in the Object Type list and the specific module you want in the Objects list, click Import, and click Close.

3. Test the new procedure by selecting the Emp# field for Jeffrey Davis's record. Access displays the message specified in the new_employee procedure, as shown here:

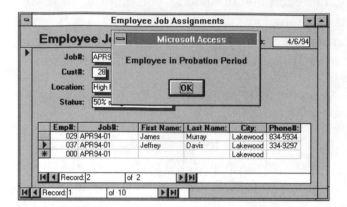

These simple modules don't begin to tap the power of Access Basic. If you are interested in pursuing this topic further, you can load one of the sample databases that came with Access and open a module to look at its code. As you'll see, you can add many procedures to the same module. Click the Next Procedure button on the toolbar to cycle through the procedures, or click the arrow to the right of the Procedure box on the toolbar to drop down a list of all the procedures in the module from which you can select a specific procedure to view. You can use the *Building Applications* manual to learn more about the procedures used in the sample databases, and you can view the topics in the Language and Technical Reference section of the Help system for online assistance.

Index

Other *Quick Course* Books

Don't miss the other titles in our *Quick Course*® series! Quality books at an unbeatable price.

A Quick Course in Windows 95
A Quick Course in Microsoft Office 95
A Quick Course in Microsoft Office 4.3 for Windows
A Quick Course in Word 6 for Windows
A Quick Course in Excel 5 for Windows
A Quick Course in PowerPoint 4 for Windows
A Quick Course in WordPerfect 6.1 for Windows
A Quick Course in Windows 3.1
A Quick Course in Windows for Workgroups
A Quick Course in DOS 6
A Quick Course in WordPerfect 5.1 for Windows
A Quick Course in Word 2 for Windows
A Quick Course in Excel 4 for Windows
A Quick Course in Paradox for Windows (1 and 4.5)

Plus more to come...

For our latest catalog, call (800) 854-3344 or fax us at (206) 641-4728, or write to us at:

Online Press Inc.
14320 NE 21st Street, Suite 18
Bellevue, WA 98007